International Students Problems

Problems

(a Study in Malaysia)

ATEFEH KAMANKESH

MOHAMED SHAFEQ

I would like to dedicate this book to my beloved parents and siblings. I'm honored to have you as my family, who brought me up with their love and give me a chance to prove and improve myself through all my walks of life.

I would like to express my sincere gratitude to my friend; Mohsen Rahmandoust for the continuous support, his patience, motivation, enthusiasm, and immense knowledge.

This book is derived from a research which was for a dissertation submitted in partial fulfillment of the requirements for the award of the degree of Master of Education (Guidance and Counseling) in Faculty of Education, Universiti Teknologi Malaysia.

CONTENTS

CHAPTER 1

INTRODUCTION

1.0 Introduction

More and more students yearn to pursue higher degrees in their respective areas of study. Since they want to study abroad they are going to face numerous challenges (Peng, 2004) such as different culture, food, environment, climate, challenges and opportunities. However the greatest problems that they face is family problems (Yeow, 2003; Gallander and Yaffe, 2000; Kenny, 1986; Linda and Jery, 1984; Terri and Fisher, 1986; Yarber and Greer, 1986; Riemer, 1974), health problems (Rosenthal, 2006; Russell and Thomson, 2008; Shute, 2007; MdYasin and Dzulkifli , 2009; Corner , 2010; Safavi and Kheiri, 2010; Seng, 2004; Inpeng, 2006), educational problems, emotional and recreational problem (Hamzeh, 2007; Farokhzadeh, 2007; Chong Abdullah, 2009; Day) and also financial problem (Haron and Issa, 2009; Worthy, et al.,2010; Fazli and Macdonald, 2008). They are a normal part of the experience of studying abroad.

According to (Ghanem and bagi, 2008) more than two-third of foreign students experiences the categories of the problems during their

1

study period. This problem is including their physical and emotional needs. Malaysia has many public universities which have a variety of different study programs. Every year a vast number of foreign students come to public universities to continue their higher education in postgraduate level. This study helps the university and the students' affair department to identify the foreign students' problems in term of demography and help the students to overcome to their problems.

1.1 Problems Origin

In an integrated world, with growing intercultural awareness, study abroad is becoming increasingly popular. Going abroad seems to be the best choice for a person looking to gain in-depth knowledge of a culture, its customs and people. Studying abroad is an excellent way to intellectual and personal growth, a way of getting to know the world. As is usually the rule, exposure to different cultures and challenges of a new academic environment makes a person more independent and mature. One learns to easily adapt to new circumstances and cultural contexts, which is a valuable life experience.

There has been a tremendous increase in the number of foreign students travelling overseas to pursuit higher education. There are various reasons to select another country for education, including, higher rank of the University, more competitive education standards, cost effective programs, and socio-political situations of the country.

Students travel abroad mainly to improve their language skills, others travel to advance their specialized studies. They are studying abroad because suitable tertiary education is unavailable altogether in their home countries. Foreign students improve their life skills and public communications and increase their confidence and self steams as a result of their new independent life experience in different culture (Sherry, et al., 2010). One of the most important things for a University is improving the rank of the University in the world which foreign students play an important role in this case. Gathering foreign students from different countries in public Universities provide a good opportunity to improve their understanding and experience sharing among students from different culture and race (Lebcir, et al., 2008).

There are many countries, which attract foreign students. One of these countries that attract a huge number of foreign students is Malaysia. Malaysia has about 600 higher education institution include community colleges to public universities with so many local and foreign students.(insider, 2008). According to Mohamed khaled Nordin, minister of higher education "Malaysia wants to be a global player and needed to share knowledge and collaboration worldwide, so their role is to produce the type of graduate that can fit into all these things". With a short glace to Malaysia states and cities you can see many students from different nationalities in this country such as (Iran, Iraq, Indonesia, Pakistan , Turkey, Somalia, Nigeria, and even as far as Belgium (Malaysian education centre). the number of students who registered in different Malaysian institutes was increased every year. the five oldest universities, each enrolled more than 20,000 by 2000,and among this Malaysians universities the privet ones and collages observed more number of foreign students around 15,000 in 1985 to about 35,000 in 1990 and to about 250,000 in 2005 (Hassan, 2006). The target public University is one of the 30 top Asians Universities; around 3000 foreign students are studying in this University Meanwhile the number of foreign students increased in public Universities every year the student's

3

problem appeared. when the students come to a foreign country for continuing higher education, they will faced by many category of problems such as health, recreational, financial, family, morality and religious, academic problem because their life style changed and it will take time to adopt to new environment, people, climate, food and culture but sometimes this problems can effect on their study and could decrease their academic performance (Din, 2002).

Malaysia has many different public and private universities such as University Malaya (UM), University Kebangsan Malaysia (UKM), Universiti Technologi Malaysia (UTM), Multi Media University (MMU); UTM is the oldest public engineering and technological university in Malaysia. The university specializes in technical studies, with separate faculties for Education, Pure Sciences, Management, and Human Resources Development. public Universities accepts many foreign students every year, the target public University has more than 20,000 students on its main campus in Johor the students who are from different nationals include Iranian, Nigerian, Indonesians, Pakistanis and other countries.

Because of the increase in the number of foreign students who come to Malaysian public Universities to pursuit higher education its necessary to the University principles and students affairs to consider the foreign students need and help them to overcome to their needs and problems. Malaysian public Universities has also seen an escalation in the number of foreign students over the recent years, and these students confront multiple challenges such as different food, climate, weather, language, environment, financial level.

1.2 Statement of the Problems

Previous studies considered problems among foreign students but didn't cover all of the problems scientifically. Furthermore its necessary to the university principles to become aware of foreign students needs and problems because if the principles don't reply the students complains it will make them disappointed and unfulfilled (Sherry, et al., 2010). Totally it can be useful to all the universities to identify the foreign student's needs and problems.

1.3 Significant of the Study

These study identify category of problems (health problems, financial problems, social relational problems, psychological social and recreational problems, psychological social relation problems, personal relationships and emotional problems, marriage and sexual problems, family problems, moral and religious problems, academic work, future career and curriculum) among foreign students in a public University of Malaysia, also students selected from foreign postgraduate students of Iran, Indonesia , Nigeria, Iraq and Pakistan who live in Skudai campus. The age and race variable were not included in demographic characteristics. Therefore finding of this study cannot be generalized to the whole the university students. This study will be useful for all the university faculties and for the body of knowledge. The study produces the new findings, which will help the other researchers in their study about the problems faced by foreign students in future.

1.3.1 University

The finding of this study can be very useful to the public universities which are going to become global universities because regarding to the finding of this book university will find a more clear vision about all of its foreign students needs and problems in different aspects of their life and studying in Malaysia and try to help the students to overcome to their problems. On the other hand, when the students problems decrease the academic performance of the students will increase also they will be ready to develop their knowledge and talents to create the new thinking's and become top in their major specifications, of curse such a active and unique students are the most important objectives for a university which is going to become a global and top university.

1.3.2 Body of the knowledge

Furthermore this study will be useful for the body of the knowledge about foreign students' problems because, before this book many researchers try to find the foreign students problems but not so deep, they just try to find a total view of the foreign students problems in overseas countries. This book is the first one that used Shafeq problem checklist to identify the foreign students' problems, this inventory consider the foreign students needs and problems very particular in most of the aspects of their life and studying through eleven categories of problems and regard to the location of this research a public University, which have a huge number of foreign students from more than ten different country of origins the validity and reliability of this book will be more real according to the number and variety of the research population sample. in addition this book results investigate the foreign students problems more precise by using Pareto principle to find the most disturbing category of problems faced by foreign students which never done before in previous studies.

1.3.3 Students

This study can be useful to the future researchers who are looking for to have a more clear vision of the foreign students problems in overseas. And also help the student office department in public Universities to identify the most disturbing problems then appropriate steps in preventing of taking correcting researcher.

1.4 Scope of the Research

This study, analyze the category of problems (health problems, financial problems, social relational problems, psychological social and recreational problems, psychological social relation problems, personal relationships and emotional problems, marriage and sexual problems, family problems, moral and religious problems, academic work, future career and curriculum) among foreign students in a public University in Malaysia. Respondents of this study are 354 foreign male and female postgraduate students from five different countries of origins (Iran, Indonesia, Nigeria, Iraq, and Pakistan) in a public University in Malaysia, who were selected through multiple sampling by the researcher. The data was collected via interview and questionnaire (June 25 and September 25 in 2010) in a public University in skudai. Pareto principles believe that the majority (about 80%) of the results is due to the contributions of a minority (about 20% of factors or agents).

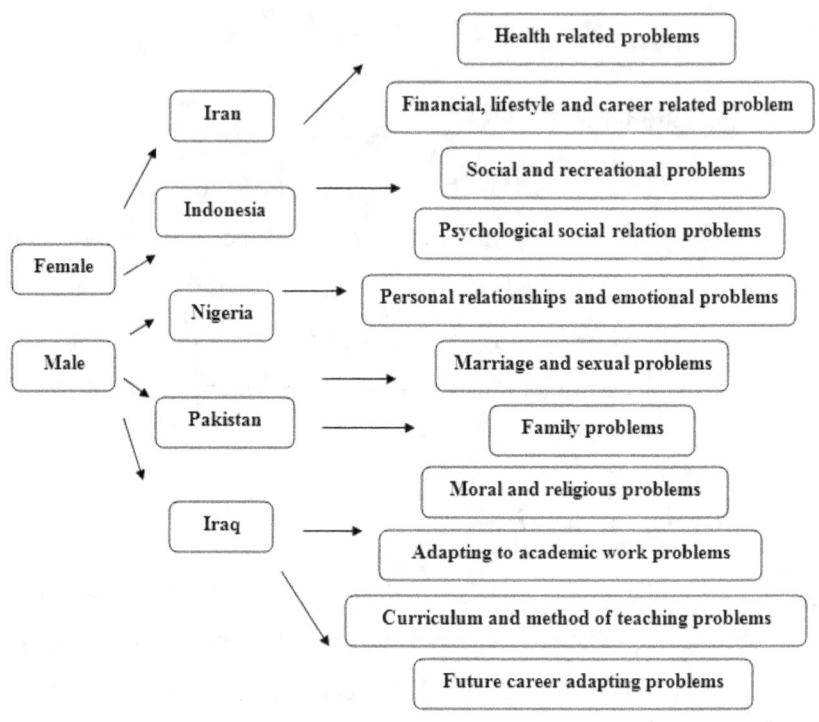

Figure 1-1 Framework

1.5 Theoretical Framework of the Study

In this study we have eleven categories of problems, we are suppose to analyze the frequency and percentage of each category of problems to find the most disturbing category of problems among foreign postgraduate students of a public University of Malaysia, furthermore to find the most disturbing category of problems in term of demography's (gender, country of origin) and also to find the most disturbing items in each category of problems in term of demography's.

There were 11 categories of problems in the questionnaire. Each category had different number of items that the participants had to choose either "Yes" if applicable or "No" if does not applicable, for each. The first category was "Health Related Problems" with sixteen items. The Second category involved 22 items regarding "Financial, Lifestyle and Career Problem". The third category was "Social and Recreational Problems" with 40 subcategories. The fourth one was "Psychological Social Relations problems" that involved 24 items in this regard. The fifth category was "Personal Relationships and Emotional Problems" with 23 items. The next category investigated "Marriage and Sexual Problems with 23 items. The seventh category tried to seek the problems related to "Family". In "Family Problem" category there were 14 items. The eighth category was "Moral and Religious Problems" which seeks understanding of this area with 15 subcategories. The ninth category of concern was "Adapting to Academic Work Problems". This category made use of 26 items to gain insight of this issue. Next category was "Future Career Adapting Problems" with 18 items of investigation. And the last category was "Curriculum and Methods of Teaching Problems" with 24 subcategories.

The findings of this study was obtained from exploratory mixed method (questioner and interview) were used to identify the most disturbing categories of problems and the most disturbing items among foreign postgraduate students from (Iran, Indonesia, Nigeria, Iraq and Pakistan) in a public University and also to gain a clear understanding of differences between problems of investigated categories based on demographic specifications (gender and country of origin). The findings

9

can be useful for both students and university to become conscious of the existent problems.

1.6 Conceptual Definitions

Conceptual definition refers to elements of the research process, in which a specific concept is defined as a measurable occurrence.

1.6.1 Problems: in this study ,problems refer to the factors that faced by foreign students (health problems, psychological social relations problems , Personal Relationships and Emotional Problems, Marriage and Sexual Problems, Family Problems, Morals and Religious Problems, Academic Work Problems, Future Career Problems, Curriculum and Method of Teaching Problems (Shafeq, 2008).

1.6.2 Foreign Students: In this study foreign students refer to students who study in a public University and come from overseas in Malaysia.

1.6.3 In this study, university is referring to a public University in Malaysia. which is one of the oldest public Universities in Malaysia. Public University supported by the government and gives admition to students from different race and nationalities.

1.7 Operational Definition

These study specific concepts that to some extent require explanations as follow:

1.7.1 University: University: in this book University refer to a public University in Malaysia.

1.7.2 Foreign students: in this study , foreign students are from five countries (Iran, Indonesia, Nigeria, Iraq and Pakistan) they are pursuing their studies in postgraduate level in a public University during data collection period.

1.7.3 Problems: students concern about unresolved sources that specify by students.

1.8 Summary

In this chapter the background of the problems, problems statement, objectives of the study, significant of the study to students and university and also body of the knowledge. In addition, definitions of operational terms were discussed. Therefore, it is clear that this study is going to identify the category of problems faced by foreign students in term of demography, and finding the highest category of problems faced by the foreign postgraduate students, the most highest disturbing items in each category of problems and the relationship between category of the problems and demography.

CHAPTER 2

LITERATURE REVIEW

2.0 Introduction

This chapter will discussed about literature review on category of problem faced by the foreign student. The discussion of the literature review will be based on the objective of the research. The objectives of this research are as follow: To identify the most disturbing category of problems (health problems, financial problems, social relational problems, psychological social and recreational problems, psychological social relation problems, personal relationships and emotional problems, marriage and sexual problems, family problems, moral and religious problems, academic work, future career and curriculum) among foreign students (Iranian, Indonesian, Nigerian, Iraqis and Pakistanis). To identify most disturbing items in each aspect of problems (health problems, financial problems, social relational problems, psychological social and recreational problems, psychological social relation problems, personal relationships and emotional problems, marriage and sexual problems, family problems, moral and religious problems, academic work, future career and curriculum). And also To identify the five most disturbing items in each aspect of problems (health problems, financial problems, social relational problems, psychological social and recreational problems, psychological social relation problems, personal relationships and emotional problems, marriage and sexual problems, family problems, moral and religious problems, academic work, future career and curriculum) in term of demography (gender, country of origin).

All the adolescents and teenagers faced with different number of challenges in their life. They should learn so many skills to overcome to their problems and experience many new things. when the students come to a foreign country for continuing higher education, they will faced by the category of problems such as health, recreational, financial, family, morality and religious, academic problem and etc (Din, 2002). Regarding to students tendency to continue higher education in overseas countries and many problems that appear to them after immigrate to the host country from the elementary days of their immigration until the end of their graduation. Many of the researchers tried to find the reasons for the foreign students problems appear and how can we prevent of this problems or help the foreign students to overcome to their problems (Rosenthal , 2006; Worthy et al., 2010; Terri and Fisher , 1986; Al khazawneh , 2010; Ghanem and Mohammad bagi , 2008).

2.1 Theoretical framework of the research

2.1.1 Maslow theory

To explore the category of problems faced by students writer try to explain about Maslow theory because, Maslow theory refer to human basic needs, this needs are the human requirement to having a good and healthy life and if the needs doesn't provide, this lack will be a causes to appear different problems for the human such as (health problems, financial problems, social relational problems, psychological social and recreational problems, psychological social relation problem, personal relationships and emotional problems, marriage and sexual problems, family problems, moral and religious problem, academic work, future career and curriculum), by regard to Maslow theory we can placed the students problems in different levels of Maslow pyramid, as you know the lowest level of Maslow pyramid is related to the human basic needs (physical and psychological needs) like health problems, sexual problems, this basic needs are the requirements to providing all other needs of the human. The second level of this pyramid is refer to security, all the people try to have security in different aspects of their life but if they couldn't provide it in their life they will faced with the problems like (moral and religious problems, family problems, psychological social and recreational problems, academic work, future career and curriculum),the third level of Maslow pyramid consider the social aspect of the human life (Friendship, intimacy, family support and having good relations, People needs to belonging and being accepted) if a person doesn't fulfil in each of this aspects he will faced the problems like (personal relationship, emotional problems and social relational problems).

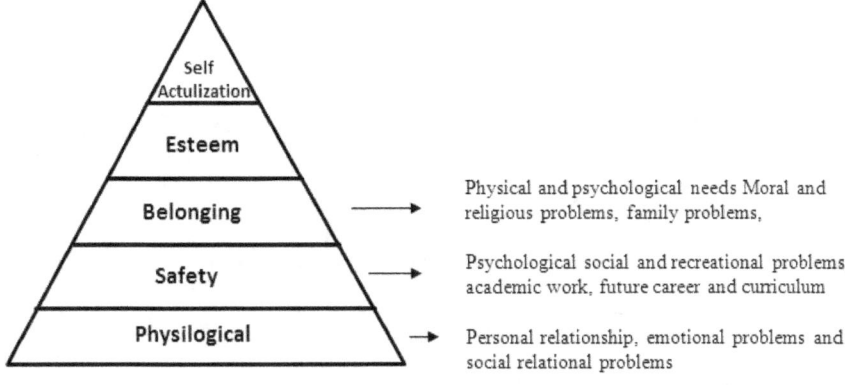

Figure 2-1 Maslow pyramid

2.1.2 Julian Rotter

He believes that we are aware of our understanding as human beings, we can influence on our experiences and collect designs to set order to our life, external strengthening plays a important role in this system but strengthens effectiveness is depends on internal cognitive factors, the external or internal sources influence on human behaviour. Persons with internal control locus are physically and mentally healthier than people with external control locus (Ratter, 1954). According to the rather theory environment can influence on people behaviour especially the persons who affected more from environment.

Ratter believes that environment can change the people behavior, because the human influence on the people and made changes to them when the people change his behavior will also change. Regard to this theory if we could solve the people problems in their environments we can help them to change themselves and their behavior and become healthier by changing the environment.

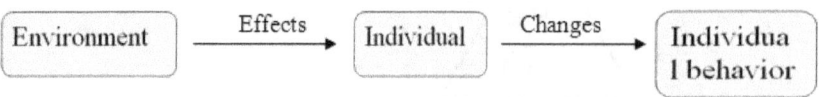

Figure 2-2 Rotter Theory

2.1.3 Erich From

From believes that being a perfect and satisfies person is in the meaning that a person used of all his potential powers and talents to creating a healthy (ego) which is the main goal for humankind his life. Regarding to achieve to this goal human need to first solve his problems then focus to explore himself to create a healthy Ego, each society most helped the residents to overcome to their problems and reach to this goal. He believes that the main causes of the individuals psychological problems is in their environment then environment is responsible to provide human needs because the source of all the human needs is in their environment.

2.2 The Most Disturbing Category of Problems among Foreign Students

One of the most disturbing problems among foreign students is health problems (Rosenthal , 2006; Russell and Thomson, 2008; Safree and Dzulkifli, 2009; Koplik and Devito, 1986) , recreational problems (Hamzeh, 2007; Farokhzadeh, 2007; Ghanem and Bagi ,2008; Basiron, 2007; Sheahila, 2008), family problems is other prominent problems

16

among foreign students (Kenny, 1986; Terri and Fisher, 1986), financial problems is the other problems which the foreign students are face with it (Sabri et al., 2008 ; Worthy et al., 2010; Ibrahim et al., 2009), adapting to academic work problems is another problem face by the foreign students (Su, 2004; Mastura Mahfar, 2007; Amir, 1983; Tinto, 1987; lee ,1997; Lewthwaite , 1997; Al khazawneh, 2010).

(Rosenthal, 2006) conduct research on category of problems among foreign students (n: 979) of undergraduate and postgraduate foreign students at Melbourne University of Australia. He found that physical health is the most disturbing problems face by students. Depression: 88% Anxiety: 81% Stress: 86%. In this research he reported about the sexual harassment, self harm, self related practices and smoking among foreign students.

Russell (2008) conduct research at the health centre of metropolitan university in Australia on (n=970) to identify the category of problems among foreign students (China, Indonesia ,Malaysia ,Singapore ,United kingdom, United State, Canada, Middle East, Africa, Europe, Latin America, South Asia) in this university, the results show that 268 person needed help,76% needed academic-educational, 60% need career-vocational,56% need personal-social-emotional need, according to the result of the categories of problems Asian students need more help in academic-educational than non Asian students.

Koplik and Devito (1986) used the Mooney problem checklist (MPCL) to compare Problems of freshmen in the classes of 1976 and 1986. A summary of their findings indicated Health and Physical Development (HDP). The students from the class of 1986 were more concerned about being overweight and not getting enough sleep, exercise, outdoor air, or sunshine. In both the 1986 and 1976 classes there were more women than men who were concerned about being tired much of the time.

Safree and Dzulkifli (2009) conduct a research at (n=120) persons, 50% male and 50% female, the undergraduate foreign students international Islamic university Malaysia (IIUM), in this study he mentioned that most of the foreign students suffer from the stress, anxiety, depression and it has the direct relation with their academic performance, in this research he found that the level of the foreign students psychological problem s such as stress, depression or anxiety have a relationship with the grade of their level of academic achievement , students in low academic achieving group reported a higher level of psychological problems such as depression, stress and anxiety as another main problems faced by the foreign students (Hamzeh, 2007; Farokhzadeh , 2007; Ghanem and Bagi , 2008 ; Chong and Abdullah , 2009).

In other research which was done by (Hamzah, 2007), to identify the categories of problem and their demography differences among four students in the Pasir Gudang zone of Johor Bahru district. (n =169) students were picked randomly for the research. MPCL was the research instrument that used, it was includes 330 items. The reliability percentage of this instrument is alpha = 0.81. The results showed that the problem most faced by the students is social and recreational activities (51.5%), adapting to academic assignments (49.8%) and personal and emotional relationships (41.0%). The items that are of least troublesome are such as health related problems (27.6%), financial, way of life and career related (31.0%) and family problems (31.3%). This book also showed differences in the main problems demographically.

Social and Recreational Activities and Morals and Religion are two main categories of problems among foreign students. According to (Basiron, 2007 ; Sheahila, 2008) In the context of university students' life, the problem most faced by the students is the failure in managing feelings and emotions effectively. In his study on (n=382) foreign students of Universiti Teknologi Malaysia (UTM) and 381 foreign students of Universiti Malaya (UM), majority of the students agreed that making residing colleges gender based is an effective way to reduce social problems in higher learning institutions.

Kenny (1986) done a research on (n=173) foreign students in University of Pennsylvania to assess the family function on first year foreign students, most of the students were agree that their family are secure base and a strong source of support, the males indicate more than females the need to turn to their parents and friends, however both female and males were satisfied with the help of their family.

The research conducted by Terry and Fisher (1986) done in Midwest University among general psychology foreign students (n=95) who where unmarried between ages 18 to 23 years old, identify the family communication and sexual behaviour of foreign students, this research shows that the quality of family communication in general is not related to family-adolescent communication about sex. There are many families with close or open communication that the sex issue is not discussed in them but also exist some families that they have a very poor quality of communication but the sex is discussed in them, it means that discussed about the sex between family and adolescents is not related to the quality of their communication in their family.

On the other hand according to the research conducted by (Sabri et al., 2008) about the financial problem among foreign student in Malaysian universities, this study done on (n = 3850) foreign students in 11 University in Malaysia include six public and five private universities. This report mentioned that the financial literacy is related positively to financial well-being, effective financial behavior=higher level of financial wellbeing, this book considered savings, goals settings, gift to family, shopping, treating friends and repaying debts in foreign students, the result of this study shows that there are not any relation between financial literacy and financial well-being . Data reveals that the male students have more financial problem than females, but most of the respondents of this study had low financial well-being and this weakness will affect their academic performance. Moreover, the students' academic performance will decrease because of their financial problems.

According to (Worthy et al., 2010) one of the most disturbing category of problems in foreign students is financial behaviour of college students, this research done in Mississippi university on (n=450) foreign students, their majors was science, art, business, education, engineering, life science, (n=332) of this foreign students were white and (n=102) African American and (n=15) from other races. The study shows that the foreign students whose their family receive public financial helps and have higher sensation-seeking score and higher adult status scores have more problematic financial problems in contrast with the students whose their family don't receive public assistance. In addition, financial problems have a direct relative to the age and gender; the older and female students have more financial problems.

The research done by Ibrahim et al. (2009) (n=133) foreign students in Kedah campus of Malaysia. To assess one of the category of the problems among foreign students which is financial literary on degree students of (marketing, Islamic banking, administration science, information service), this study shows that the degree students have a very poor financial knowledge and they cannot manage their money. On the other hand, this book indicates that the weakness of the students in money management skill is not related to the gender or family background or the major of the students.

Hundred and twenty foreign students residing in collage thirteen of UTM campus were picked randomly to participate in this study to identify the highest category of problems. According to book results the categories of problem most faced by students are academic and future career (16.4%) followed by adapting to academic assignments (11.80%) and moral and religious factors (10.7%). Categories of problem that least trouble students are family problems (5.8%) followed by curriculum and teaching and learning techniques (5.6%) and health related problems (5.2%) (Su, 2004).

Another research showed that most of the students around (80.0%) experience stress due to lack of knowledge on having a good command of English Language , (93.3%) experience stress due to preparing for career life, (83.3%) for career challenged , (80.0%) for other career opportunities and (86.7%) for skills of writing a resume .

Mahfar (2007) and Amir (1983) stated that students with clear information will be able to achieve success and excel in their future career. Thus, students are usually tensed up when they do not have comprehensive preparation for career life. In addition to that, competition in job opportunities is getting more difficult nowadays with criteria for job specifications increased by industries giving additional stress to students.

Tinto (1987) posited that individual characteristics, prior experiences, and goal commitments along with the individual's integration into the academic and social systems of the institution directly influence upon students retention and success. Included in this process are aspects of the student's life both past and present. Other factors along with integration or the inability to integrate into the social environment of the college affected upon student attrition and retention. These were external factors such as cost and benefits, individual characteristics, and goal commitment.

Lee (1997) identity the top five most problems faced by foreign students in classroom in an American universities who the English language is their second or third language, this problems was include poor listening ability, differences in cultural background, neglect in oral communication skills, weakness in vocabulary and writing.

According to Lewthwaite (1997) the reasons that lead to problematic foreign students are adopt to their new academic, social, cultural and linguistic environment, from the (n=12) respondents to this research were six female and six male, foreign students in Massy University from Indonesia, Thailand, Japan and Taiwan, the most frustration for all this foreign students was the lack of self confidence in their English language ability to contribute in seminars or lecturers.

There are many studies around problems faced by foreign students especially academic problems, in one research which has done by (Al-khazawneh, 2010) in (n=10) Arab postgraduate students (five Jordanians, two Iraqi, two Libyans and one Yamanies) between the ages

(25 to 40) in the business program of COB in University Utara Malaysia. According to the respondents major, the ability of writing and speaking in English will be very important for them because this ability could increase their business skills. The study shows that all this students had problems in vocabulary, grammar, organization of ideas, spelling and referencing, most of the respondents of this study maintained that their main problem is in vocabulary.

2.3   Category of problems in terms of demography's:

Regarding to some students who comes to Malaysia from different country of origins most of them faced health problems because of the different climate ,foods (Rosenthal, 2006), all foreign male and female students from different country of origins experience similar significant of problems (Brunder, 1979; Better, 1980) ,and there is no different in the amount of the students complaints based on their gender or country of origin (Yeung, 1980; Poorshaghaghi 1992; sonari, 1998). But some findings shows foreign male students faced more problems in compared with female students (Kuang–wu, 2000; Razavi, 1988; Shahmirzadi, 1988). One of these problems is emotional problems which can be a reason to students physical or mental illness because they separated from their hometown, family, friends and their belongings, most of the foreign students experienced homesickness and loneliness in their first semesters (Russell, 2008). (Seng et al, 2004) mentioned in (Peng, 2006) to identify the level of stress among students in a college in Malaysia ,the results showed that level of stress experienced by the respondents is very high especially regarding matters such as adapting, financial and academic results. According to this book result female

23

students were more prone to stress than male students. Besides that, male students were also found to be able to handle stress better than female students.

In this study researcher wants to identify the most disturbing categories of problems among postgraduate foreign students based on their country of origins and their gender, most of the previous researchers on different communities show that gender have a effective roles in individuals feelings and decisions in their life (Brooks-Gunn et al., 1994; Caspi and Moffitt, 1991; Conger and Elder, 2001). As regard every students come to Malaysia from different country most of them faced health problems because of the different climate, foods (Rosenthal, 2006), foreign male and female students experience similar significant of problems (Brunder,1979; Ramirez Better, 1980), and there is no different in the amount of the students complaints based on their gender (Yeung, 1980; Poorshaghaghi, 1992; sonari, 1998). But some findings shows international male students faced more problems in compared with female students (Kuang–wu, 2000; Razavi, 1988; Shahmirzadi, 1988).

2.3.1 Category of problems in term of Gender

Classification the challenges among foreign male and female students can assist to reconnoiter and to prevent the future problems. Because of the importance of the foreign student's problems, many previous researchers try to categorized this problems to several highlighter items to create a clear picture of the different foreign student's problems based on their gender in order to find solutions to prevents or overcome to these problems (Manese et al.,1988).

2.3.1.1 Different level of emotional problems among male and female student

According to (Kenny, 1986) about the family problem he mentioned that the female students like to seek out the help of their parents and their friend quite a bit, while the male students indicate that they were like to turn to parents and friends more than a moderate amount. Males described themselves as more likely than the females to work out problems on their own. Also in this study the significant relationship between assertion and characteristics of the parent relationship was found only for the females' sample. In a similar research (Worthy et al., 2010) mentioned that in assessing the financial behavior of the foreign students, the older female students have more financial problem. On the other hand (Tamblyn, 1974) done a research about the Annotated Bibliography of research on foreign students in the U.S, in this research he maintained that female students are more emotional and more financially secure than males. In addition, females were significantly more likely than males to endorse "modern" work roles for women, while males tended to endorse "traditional" roles for women that involved homemaking and childrearing. The percentage of females endorsing modern attitudes increased with their level of education. It is suggested that the more modern values of educated Arab women may result in conflicts between men and women and between more and less educated women (Abdalla et al., 1984).

Based on a T-test which has done on a number of foreign students in both gender to determine their overall strengths 7adjustment problems based on their gender, the average of their overall strengths of the seven adjustment problems is significantly lower for male students in compare with female students in four adjusting problems (accommodation problems ,health problems, academic problems and advising problem), (Kuang-wu, 2000).

According to (Sawir et al., 2007) when the students come to overseas they faced emotional problem because of loneliness, different language and culture friends and classmates they couldn't find anyone to be close to her to share their needs and problems, especially this problem is more usual among female foreign students, because females are more controlled by their emotions and more need to share when they are in challenge (Brooks-Gunn et al., 1994; Caspi and Moffitt, 1991; Conger, and Elder, 2001),in opposite to his research (Tamblyn, 1974) done a research about the annotated Bibliography of Research on foreign Students in the U.S, in this research he maintained that Female students are more emotional in compare with their male classmates. furthermore one of the previous researches show that female students like to seek out the help of their parents and their friend quite a bit, while the male students indicate that they were like to turn to parents and friends more than a moderate amount. Males described themselves as more likely than the females to work out problems on their own.

2.3.1.2 Different level of financial problems among male and female students

Also in this study the significant relationship between assertion and characteristics of the parent relationship was found only for the females' sample (Kenny, 1986) ,on the other hand another serious problems among foreign students is financial problems (sabri et al., 2008; Worthy et al.,2010; Ibrahim et al., 2009) but the researches show the level of financial problems is not the same in both gender, because of the necessary of this issue with a short glance to the previous research you can find many researchers who emphasize on foreign students financial problems, (Worthy et al., 2010) mentioned that in assessing the financial behaviour of the foreign students, the female older students have more financial problem. On the other hand (Tamblyn, 1974) done a research about the Annotated Bibliography of Research on International Students in the U.S, in this research he maintained Female students are more financially Secure than males.

2.3.1.3 Different level of recreational problems among male and female students

Based on (Hatman, 1968) study of community college freshmen and sophomores, the future: vocational and educational area ranked second highest in terms of serious problems but last for females. Social-psychological relations ranked third highest as a serious problem for female but only cighth highest for males. Males indicated that the least number of serious problems were in the areas of social and recreational activities and curriculum and teaching procedures. Females indicated that their least serious problems were in the areas concerning the future: vocational and educational, and finances: living conditions and employment. Hatman (1968) also noted that males admitted to having more problems than females and a greater willingness to discuss their problems with professionals. According to (Burkes , 1995) females students have more problem than males in academic, social, cultural and related adjustment, issues confronted by African American undergraduate studying at West Virginia University.

Mayes and MC Conatha (1982) found about the favourite Social and Recreational Activities that men felt awkward making a date more than women and women wanted to improve themselves and travel more than men. Opposite to the men, women felt too easily hurt and complained of speaking without thinking and they have complained of loneliness, felt inferior, and they were taking things too seriously, were moody, and experienced lack of self-confidence (Mayes and MC Conatha ,1982).

Mayes and MC Conatha (1982) used the MPCL and found that about the Social and Recreational Activities (SRA). More students in the class of 1986 indicated concerns regarding personal appearance and not having enough time to them. In both classes, more men than women felt awkward making a date, and more women than men wanted to improve themselves and travel.

2.3.1.4 Different level of health problems among male and female students

On the other side a research conducted by (Seng et al., 2004) mentioned in (Peng, 2006) to identify the level of stress among students in a college in Malaysia showed that level of stress experienced by the respondents is very high especially regarding matters such as adapting, financial and academic results. The subject of the research showed that the female students were more prone to stress than male students were. Besides that, male students also found to be able to handle stress better than female students were. Gender difference in the reported problems of the Pennsylvania university students were examined by (Ginsberg, 1980) using the Mooney problem Check List and the college student

Questionnaire. He found that the female students reported more problems in the area of academic demands than in the area of social skills. The male students reported the opposite order.

The research conducted by (Seng et al, 2004) mentioned in (Peng, 2006) to identify the level of stress among students in a college in Malaysia for the academic session of 2003/04 showed that level of stress experienced by the respondents is very high especially regarding matters such as adapting, financial and academic results. The subject of the research which was (n=393) students consisting of 159 male students and 234 female students showed that the female students were more prone to stress than male students. Besides that, male students were also found to be able to handle stress better than female students.

More women than men felt too easily hurt and complained of speaking without thinking. In the class of 1976, more women than men complained of loneliness, and in the class of 1986, more women felt inferior, and more men wanted to be popular. And also Women more that men indicated that they were taking things too seriously, were moody, and experienced lack of self-confidence (Mayes and Mc Conatha, 1982).

2.3.1.5 Different level of academic problems among male and female students

Gender differences in the reported problems of 116 students at the University of Pennsylvania were examined by (Ginsberg, 1980) using the Mooney Problem Check List (MPCL) and the college student questionnaire. He found that the female students reported more problems in the area of academic demands than in the area of social skills. The male students reported the opposite order. In another research which used the Mooney Problem Check List (MPCL) and done by Hatman's (1968) study of community college freshmen and sophomores, shows that "The future: vocational and educational area problems ranked as second highest in terms of serious problems but last for females. Social-psychological relations ranked as third highest, serious problems faced by female and eighth highest problems faced by males. Males indicated that the least number of serious problems were in the areas of social and recreational activities and curriculum and teaching procedures. Females indicated that their least serious problems were in the areas concerning the future: vocational and educational, and finances: living conditions and employment. Hatman also noted that males admitted to having more problems than females and a greater willingness to discuss their problems with professionals.

Burkes (1995) designed a study to determine academic, social, cultural, and related adjustment issues confronted by African American undergraduate studying at West Virginia University. Using the MPCL, she found that females indicated more problems than males in these areas.

2.3.2 Category of problems in term of students Country of origins

Specifically, African students encountered more difficulties in total adjustment and in more problem areas than the other groups. Asian students expressed the greatest difficulties in the English language area. Middle-Eastern students expressed the fewest difficulties in the financial aid and English language areas. Students who were self-supported had more problems than students who were financially supported by their families in the orientation services, financial aid, and placement services. Also, the study showed that students who were supported by their families experienced more difficulties (Hilal, 1987).

2.3.2.1 Different level of academic problems among students from different country of origins

According to Fleming (1984), developmental education programs focus on the academic and personal needs of the black students; however, the developmental process is too often overshadowed by race. Race takes precedence over normal development. She concluded that African American students do not have the luxury of concentrating on normal developmental issues.

2.3.2.2 Different level of recreational problems among male and female students

Day et al., (1986) according to the research which don in American university of Beirut foreign students, 198 Lebanese (age 18 to 25 years old) and 75 foreign students (age 20 to 35 years old), the most circulate item for Lebanese were in social and recreational activities area and for the foreign students were in the curriculum and teaching area.

Studies on race and personal problems showed different personal problem profiles among races. (Greene and Kester, 1970) published the results of their research done at Chabot Community college in Hayward California. Greene used the MPCL and Personal Integration and Omnibus Personality Inventories to sample problem of black, Chicano and "other "students in a college. It should be noted that the Chicano students refused to participate in the study. Statistical analysis of comparisons made between the black group and the "other" group showed no significant difference on the personal integration and Omnibus Personality Inventories. Differences were found on the Mooney Problem Check List in the area of finances, living conditions and employment. Greene concluded that black students had problems that were different from those experienced by other students.

2.4 Summery

The purpose of this study is categorized the students problems in term of demography in a public University in Malaysia, In this chapter we used the previous studies to explain the category of problem(health problems, financial problems, social relational problems, psychological social and recreational problems, psychological social relation problem, personal relationships and emotional problems, marriage and sexual problems, family problems, moral and religious problem, academic work, future career and curriculum) in term of demography (gender, country of origin) the result of the researches showed that the categories of problems most faced by foreign students are adapting to academic work problems, health problems, financial problems, family problems and recreational problems.

CHAPTER 3

RESEARCH METHODOLOGY

3.0 Introduction

In this book, we are able to investigate and categorize the foreign student's problems who are studying in postgraduate level in a public University in Malaysia and help the university to identify the categories of the problems faced by the foreign students and also help the students to overcome to their problems.

In this chapter, the methodology of research will be discussed, including design of the study, location of the study, instruments, population and sample, data collection methods, data analysis methods and summary.

3.1 Design of the book

Since the purpose of the book focus on the categories of the problems, foreign postgraduate students selected to be respondents for this study. In this study exploratory method was used. The exploratory method was used because it is economical in saving time, labor and money and can use it for a big group of respondents in the short period. This study is able to ascertain the categories of problems in terms of demography. In this book writer try to use exploratory method because the topic of the book is new and need to explore the aspects of the study quantitatively and qualitatively by using interview and questionnaire.

Exploratory Method

Exploratory research provides insides into and an understanding of, the problem confronting the researcher. Exploratory research is conducted because a problem has not been clearly defined. Exploratory research provides insight and comprehension into an issue or situation. Exploratory research can help determine the research design, best way(s) to collect data.

Table 3.1 the design of the research

Research Design		
Quantitative research		**Qualitative research**
Shafeq Problem Check List (MPCL)		Interview
Part A	Part B	Open-ended
Demographic part	Category of problems	Questionnaire

3.1.1 Quantitative research paradigm

Quantitative research is all about quantifying relationships between variables. To express the relationship between variables using effect statistics, such as correlations, relative frequencies, or differences between means. In quantitative research, aim is to determine the relationship between things in a population. Quantitative research designs are either descriptive (subjects usually measured once) or experimental (subjects measured before and after a treatment).One of the main points about the quantitative paradigm is that we can use it for assessment the human behaviors and social phenomenon . Personal meanings and feelings. One of the main processes in quantitative paradigm is sampling process (Easton, 2010/2009).

In this book Shafeq Problem Check List (SPCL) was used as a quantitative method. SPCL is a modified version of Mooney problem checklist which was piloted on the targeted nationality in the university, its consists of 11 different categories of problems (health problems, financial problems, social relational problems, psychological social and recreational problems, psychological social relation problem, personal relationships and emotional problems, marriage and sexual problems, family problems, moral and religious problem, academic work, future career and curriculum).also have items to measure number of disturbing items in statistical technique such as percentages.

In this book quantitative method play the main role to finding the most highlighted problems faced by international students because the quantitative instrument and considered all the foreign students' problems in different aspect of their life.

3.1.2 Qualitative research paradigm

Qualitative research is intended to penetrate to the deeper significance that the subject of the research ascribes to the topic being researched. It involves an interpretive, naturalistic approach to its subject matter and gives priority to what the data contribute to important research questions or existing information (Denzin, 1994).In this book writer do the open-ended interview on 10 persons, researcher choose two persons from each country of origins based on the study target grope nationalities and gender (Iran, Indonesia, Nigeria, Iraq, Pakistan) and the interview was consist of open ended questions.

3.2 Population and sampling

Multi sampling (stratified sampling, systematic sampling) was used to determine the sample of respondents of these study. First, stratified sampling was used; stratified sampling involves selecting research participants based on their memberships in a particular subgroup or stratum. (Vanderstoep and Johnstone, 2009).

In order to determine the sample size Kerjeci and Morgan (1970) sample size table was used the total number of students from five countries (Iran, Indonesia, Nigeria, Iraq, Pakistan) is 1908. The distribution number of students from Iran (N=1320), Indonesia (N=260), Nigeria (N=122), Iraq (109), Pakistan (N=97). Iranian contribute 62.4% of the population, the sample size for Iranian is 221, Indonesian 43 (12.1%), Nigeria 30 (8.5%), Iraq 30 (8.5%), Pakistan 30 (8.5%).

According to Morgan table, through the total number of foreign postgraduate students n=1908, from (Iran, Indonesia, Nigeria, Iraq, Pakistan) the volume of sample must be 354 persons. This sample table shows the volume stratified of foreign postgraduate students according to their country of origin.

Table 3.2 the stratified sampling of respondents

No	Nationality	Population	Percentage	Sample
1	Iran	1320	62.4%	221
2	Indonesia	260	12.1%	43
3	Nigeria	122	8.5	30
4	Iraq	109	8.5	30
5	Pakistan	97	8.5	30
6	Total	1908	100%	354

Then Systematic sampling was used as a second sampling method. writer selected the respondents systematically from the list of students names, received from School of Postgraduate Students (SPS). In order to choose the respondents the researcher write the students name one by one on a piece of paper then put all the papers on a bowl then accidently take the papers and choose the respondents.

Systematic sampling

Systemic sampling was used as a second method. The school of postgraduate students give the list of students according to the student's country of origin. Based on this name list, they were systematically picked randomly. The researcher write the numbers 1,2,3,...9,0 on each piece of papers. Each piece of paper is rolled and put into a box. The researcher picked a number X, then sample will be X, 1X, 2X, 3X ...9X and 0X were chosen from the list of students according to their country of origin. This processed is completed when the number of required sample is fulfilled.

3.3 Location of the research

The study done in a public University of Malaysia based on the population of all the foreign postgraduate students who are studying in this public University. Researcher break up the sample of the study to five country of origin which has the highest number of postgraduate students (more than 30 students) in a public University include (Iran, Indonesia, Nigeria, Iraq, Pakistan).

3.4 Research Instruments

In this exploratory research used both qualitative and quantitative method.

3.4.1 Qualitative method

In this study open-ended questions used as the qualitative instrument participated ten respondents, two people from each country of origins (Iran, Indonesia, Nigeria, Iraq and Pakistan) were selected randomly. Interview done to identify the most disturbing problems of foreign postgraduate students in each department of a public University in Malaysia.

Open-ended questions asked to the participants face to face and then interviewees answer the questions in the answer sheet each interview section take times around twenty minutes. After collecting the interviews results the researcher try to analyze the interviews manually to identify the highest problems among foreign postgraduate students.

The interview is consisting of different parts as follow:

➢ Problems faced by students when they come to university for the first time until now

➢ Teaching / supervision / lecturers

➢ Graduate school

➢ Health centre

➢ Conclusion

Table 3.3 shows Symbols used in this interview

No	Respondents	Amount	Symbol
1	Iran first respondent	1	Iran R1
2	Iran second respondent	1	Iran R2
3	Indonesia first respondent	1	Indonesia R1
4	Indonesia second respondent	1	Indonesia R2
5	Nigeria first respondent	1	Nigeria R1
6	Nigeria second respondent	1	Nigeria R2
7	Iraq first respondent	1	Iraq R1
8	Iraq second respondent	1	Iraq R2
9	Pakistan first respondent	1	Pakistan R1
10	Pakistan second respondent	1	Pakistan R2
	Total	10	-

3.4.2 Quantitative method

In quantitative method a set of Mooney Problem Checklist(1957) modified by Syed Shafeq (2008) was used to identify the most disturbing category of problems and most disturbing Items in each category of problems faced by foreign students.

Shafeq problem checklist (2008) is including 232 items and 11 category of problems. The entire questioner consisted of 242 questions, including two Parts, Part A and B. Part A is including ten demographic questions that are regarding to the respondents bio data, the respondent is required to fill in the blanks or tick at the given boxes.

Part A: Demographic information

Part A is consisting of 10 demographic questions. The 10 demographic questions are related to personal and academic background such as gender, nationality, semester and level of study and status.

Part B (SPCL):

Part B is including 232 questions in eleven parts and it has regarded the problems by categories. The 11 categories are as follow (health problems, financial problems, social relational problems, psychological social and recreational problems, psychological social relation problems, personal relationships and emotional problems, marriage and sexual problems, family problems, moral and religious problems, academic work, future career and curriculum), the questions are delivered in the format of English, considering the better understanding of students. The sub questions of each category are related to the problems in different aspects. Categories of problems: This section contained 11 questions with sub questions. This section is to investigate postgraduate foreign student's problems.

Table 3.4 Category of problems and the number of items in each sub title

No	Category of Problems	Item
1	Health and Physical Development (HDP)	16
2	Financial and Living Conditions, and Employment (FLE)	22
3	Social and Recreational Activities (SRA)	27
4	Social Psychological Relation(SPR)	24
5	Personal Psychological Relations (PPR)	23
6	Courtship, Sex, and Marriage (CSM)	23
7	Home and Family(HF)	14
8	Moral and Religious(MR)	15
9	Adjustment to College Work(ACW)	26
10	Future Vocational and Educational (FVE)	18
11	Curriculum and Teaching procedure (CTP)	24
	Total number of Items	232

3.4.2.1 Scaling

Scaling is the branch of measurement that involves the construction of an instrument that associates qualitative constructs with quantitative metric units. Scaling evolved out of efforts in psychology and education to measure "immeasurable" constructs like health and self esteem. In many ways, scaling remains one of the most arcane and misunderstood aspects of social research measurement. In addition, it attempts to do one of the most difficult of research tasks -- measure abstract concepts.

Scaling of category of Shafeq Problem Check List (SPCL) is consist of YES or NO, according to the Shafeq Problem Check List respondents are required to mark Yes=1 or No=0.

3.4.2.2 Manual Scoring

Quantitative data are represented in the form of scores. SPCL consists of 232 items in 11 categories. Based on Farlex clipart collection 2003-2008 Princeton University, scoring is evaluation of performance by assigning a grade or score. Each category of problems has different items. By calculating the percentage and the efficiency of the items in each category of problems a comparison between the percentage of the highest and the lowest percentage was intended to make. The highest percentage of each category is the most disturbing items which were scored by students' answers.

To calculate manual scoring of the Shafeq Problem Check List (2008) we will use of this Formula:

X= (total number of students × number of items tick of each sub scale) ÷ (total number of students × total number of items) × 100

3.4.2.3 Reliability & validity based on pilot study

Reliability is the "consistency" or "repeatability" of your measures, according to (William and Trochim, 2008). The reliability of a research instrument concerns the extent to which the instrument yields the same results on repeated trials. Although unreliability is always present to a certain extent, there will generally be a good deal of consistency in the results of a quality instrument gathered at different times. The tendency toward consistency found in repeated measurements is referred to as reliability (Carmines and Zeller, 1979).

This fact makes it very important that the researcher in the social sciences and humanities determine the reliability of the data gathering instrument to be used (Willmott and Nuttall, 1975). Shafeq used Cronbach's alpha and Shafeq Problem Check List in 2008 , on (n=301) students, the result shows 0.78 to 0.81 percent reliability to this instrument (MPCL). According to the pilot study which the researcher done on a sample of my research target group the coronbach alpha for Shafeq Problem Check List separated in each category is as follow:

Table 3.5 Cronbach's alpha for Shafeq Problem Check List

Categories of problems	Cronbach's alpha
Health and Physical Development	0.67
Financial and Living Conditions, and Employment	0.73
Social and Recreational Activities	0.74
Social Psychological Relation	0.81

Personal Psychological Relations	0.81
Courtship, Sex, and Marriage	0.73
Home and Family	0.80
Moral and Religious	0.59
Adjustment to College Work	0.75
Future Vocational and Educational	0.77
Curriculum and Teaching procedure	0.77
Total number of Items	0.87

The Cronbach's alpha coefficient for Health Related Problems was 0.67, Financial and Lifestyle Problems was 0.73, Social and Social and Recreational Problems was 0.74, Psychological Social Relation Problems was 0.81, Personal Relationships and Emotional Problems was 0.81, Marriage and Sexual Problems was 0.73, Family Problems was 0.80, Moral and Religious Problems was 0.59, Adapting to Academic Work Problems was 0.75, the Future Career Adapting Problems was 0.77, Curriculum and Method of Teaching Problems was 0.77 and finally total of Cronbach's Alpha coefficient for all categories is 8.17. According to Nunnally and Benstein (1994), minimum acceptable coefficient is 0.70. Hence, all the constructs have reliability of more than 0.70 which implied that all the categories from the constructs were statistically reliable and none of the items needed to be deleted. It was concluded that the reliability of the instrument was high

Validity is the extent to which the interpretations of the results of a test are warranted, which depends on the particular use the test is intended to serve. Validity can be defined as the degree to which a test measures what it is supposed to measure. There are three basic

44

approaches to the validity of tests and measures as shown by (Mason and Bramble, 1989). There are two parts to the evaluation of the construct validity of a test. First and most important, the theory underlying the construct to be measured must be considered. Second, the adequacy of the test in measuring the construct is evaluated (Mason and Bramble, 1989). The researcher defines postgraduate foreign students' problems such as health, financial, recreational, educational problems etc. This definition is based upon the researcher's own observations. Furthermore, the researcher cannot find evidence in the research literature supporting the postgraduate foreign students' problem as defined here. Using this information, the validity of the postgraduate foreign student's problems itself can be questioned. In this case, the researcher must reformulate the previous definition of the postgraduate foreign students' problem.

Based on the pilot study some changes was done in three parts of the questioner based on understanding of the respondents the changes are in marriage and sexual category of problems and moral and religious category of problems as follow, in category number six (marriage and sexual problems) in item number 129, girlfriend add to boyfriend, because the respondents were include both gender. second in category number eight (moral and religious problems) in item number 150, mosque and church added to temple and also in item number 153 of this category, words Quran and Injil added to bible because the respondents were consist of different religion .In other words, the researcher must show that the construct being measured is not the same as one that was measured under a different name. In this book this procedure is used to assess the reliability of the data.

3.5 Research Procedure

In this process first the writer tried to set the objectives of the study. Setting the objectives of the study is significant in determining what sorts of information are needed to be gathered. In order to design the methodology of the study the literature was reviewed and existing resources of students, time, and finance were examined. Finally, preliminary tabulations and sampling as well as program analysis was done. Then the researcher done the sampling and select the suitable survey method. The survey and the samples were piloted and the questionnaire and samples were improved based on the results of the pilot study. Before doing the main survey a brief interviews were done and explanatory letters for postal questionnaire was sent. When the survey carried out, the researcher edit, code and decided the final record. Then the data was recorded and analyzed based on the target data processing method. Eventually the researcher reported the findings of the study based on the study.

For the purpose of this study, postgraduate foreign students in 2010/2011, with English language are selected. In qualitative approach, interviews were conducted in semester I, 2010. Brief explanations about the objectives of the research were given to the respondents. Each interview lasted 20 minutes and the same questions were asked from all the students. The interviews were conducted in respondents' offices.

In quantitative approach, a brief explanation about the objectives of the research, the aim of the questionnaire, and the way to answer the questionnaire were stated in the instruction letter. The questionnaires distributed among the students in semester II, 2011 and 45 minutes were given to the students to answer the questionnaire. The questionnaire was consisted of two parts: Part A included students' profile and Part B included 11 categories of problems that each one had various items. Students were asked to answer the questions in the provided space in part A. If the personal information was not relevant, students could leave it blank. Also in part B which consisted of different items they should tick (√) the relevant one.

The writer obeyed some regulation while conducting the book; such as below:

- Tried to have good relationship with the respondents

- Explained clearly about objective of the research for the respondents

- Determined comfortable location for explanation.

    to the respondents.

3.6 Data Process and Analysis

Data processing:

Data collected were processed by application of Statistical Package for Social Sciences (SPSS) to facilitate understanding and find the percentages of five highest category of problems. Data and information, which are getting from questionnaire, will be quantitatively analyzed.

Regarding to too many items in each category of problems the researcher must find a solution to summarize the data to having the more exacts report, after collecting data I used Pareto principle to find the most disturbing items in each category of problems, Pareto principle states that, roughly 80% of the effects come from 20% of the causes. According to this principle and study questions writer find five most disturbing items in each category of problems faced by postgraduate foreign students. In order to analysis the students' demography descriptive analysis will used.

3.7 Summary

This chapter discussed about the research design, population and sampling, instruments, procedures of data collection and the procedures of data analysis. In this study used exploratory method by using questionnaires to collect data. Descriptive statistics such as frequency and percentage will used to answer the objectives of the study. The results of the study would be discussed in depth in Chapter 4 and to be compared with previous study if the results are consistent.

CHAPTER 4

RESULTS

4.0 Introduction

This chapter represents the results of the study, obtained from the interview and questioners collected back from the foreign postgraduate students in UTM. First of all the interview reports, after that the questioner followed by foreign postgraduate students will analysis.

4.1 Analysis of qualitative report

In this interview participated ten respondents, two people from each country of origins (Iran, Indonesia, Nigeria, Iraq and Pakistan) were selected randomly. Interview done to identify the most disturbing problems of foreign postgraduate students in each department of university. Open-ended questions asked to the participants face to face and then interviewees answer the questions in the answer sheet each interview section take times around twenty minutes. After collecting the interviews results the researcher try to analyze the interviews manually to identify the highest problems among postgraduate foreign students in a university.

The interview is consisting of different parts as follow:

➢ Problems faced by students when they come to university for the first time until now.

➢ Teaching / supervision / lecturers

➢ Graduate school

➢ Health centre

➢ Conclusion

Table 4.1 Symbols used in this interview

No	Respondents	Amount	Symbol
1	Iran first respondent	1	Iran R1
2	Iran second respondent	1	Iran R2
3	Indonesia first respondent	1	Indonesia R1
4	Indonesia second respondent	1	Indonesia R2
5	Nigeria first respondent	1	Nigeria R1
6	Nigeria second respondent	1	Nigeria R2
7	Iraq first respondent	1	Iraq R1
8	Iraq second respondent	1	Iraq R2
9	Pakistan first respondent	1	Pakistan R1
10	Pakistan second respondent	1	Pakistan R2
	Total	10	-

4.1.1 Most disturbing Problems faced by foreign postgraduate students

No	Problems	Respondents
1	Adopt to new foods	(Indonesia R1, Nigeria R1, Iran R1, Yamane R1, R2)
2	Accommodation	(Indonesia R1, Nigeria R1, R2, Iran R1,R2, Iraq R1, R2,Pakistan R1)
3	Transportation	(Iran R1 , Nigeria R1)
4	Single entry visa	(Indonesia R1, Iran R2 ,Iraq R2)
5	Climate	(Nigeria R1,R2 ,Iraq R1)
6	Lack of on-campus recreational facilities	(Iran R2,indonesis R1,Nigeria R1,Pakistan R2)
7	Lack of financial support to foreign students	(Nigerian R2,Indonesian R1,iranianR1,Pakistan R2)
8	Lack of lecturers English and teaching method skills	(Iran R1,R2, Nigeria R1, R2,Indonesia R2,Iraq R1)
9	Lack of enough professional staffs in Graduate school	(Iran R2, China R1)
10	Lack of specialist doctor in Health centre	(Iran R1,R2, Indonesia R 1,R2,Iraq R2, Nigeria R 2)
11	Lack of enough medical equipment in health centre	(Iran R2, Indonesia R 1)
12	Lack of effective medicine given by doctors	(Iraq R2, Indonesia R2, Nigeria R 2, Iran R1)

The main problems were, adopted with the new foods (Indonesia R1, Nigeria R1, Iran R1, Yamane R1, R2), accommodation (Indonesia R1, Nigeria R1, R2, Iran R1, R2, Iraq R1, R2, Pakistan R1) transportation (Iran R1 , Nigeria R1) , single entry visa (Indonesia R1, Iran R2 , Iraq R2) , climate (Nigeria R1, R2 ,Iraq R1) , lack of on-campus recreational facilities (Iran R2 ,Indonesia R1, Nigeria R1, Pakistan R2), lack of financial support to foreign students (Nigerian R2, Indonesian R1, IranianR1,Pakistan R2).

Most of the respondents complains about hostels principles, they announced that principles make double standard between local and foreign students (Nigeria R1, Iran R 1,R 2).In one of the female hostels There are more than 5 vacant rooms but principles don't allow students to stay there (Nigeria R1 and Pakistan R2),another students complains about hostel safety and cleanliness (Nigeria R1, Indonesia R1,Iraq R1,R2). The reports show that during last semester three times men from outside enter to females hostel (Iranian community), last two month ago a man who was wear staffs clothes enter to female hostel and had threatened a girl with knife (Iran R1).

Another complains was related to internet access in hostels (Indonesia R2, Iraq R1, R2, Nigeria R1). Some of the respondents complains was related to transportation system in University (Nigeria R1, Indonesia R1, R2, Iraq R 1, R2). There are no punctual bus drivers (Nigeria R1).some of the bus drivers cannot speak English and some of them don't know University environment and departments exactly such as career and counseling centre of University (Iraq R2). The adequacy of bus services also is very limit (Indonesia R2) furthermore many of the students have request to consider bus services in campus during holidays (Iran R2. Nigeria R1, R2, Iraq R1).

Also we received some complained regarding University restaurant foods (Iraq R1, R2, Iran R1, Nigeria R1, R2). Spicy and sweet foods served in dirty and noisy restaurants which are full of cats and mosquito (Iran R1).

Furthermore most of the foreign students are unsatisfied about the recreational facilities and programs in University (Iran R2, Indonesia R1, Nigeria R1, Pakistan R2), there is some vocational trips for students in University but this programs are just for local students not foreign students (Pakistan R2).

Most of the complaints in this part was related to lecturers Malay language usage in the class (Iran R2, Nigeria R1, R2) and also most of the students believe that University lecturers must improve their knowledge and make it up to date (Indonesia R2, Iran R1), the lecturers must introduce some related references to students (Indonesia R2, Iraq R1, Nigeria R1, Iran R 2).

University lecturers are professional but their English ability is very weak (Iran R 2) lecturers most also introduce new references to students to improve their knowledge (Iraq R2). Most of the lecturers and supervisor try to do financial support just for local students but its clearly appear that the foreign students study more than local students (Nigeria R1). There is no support from the university or supervisors to the students to participate in conferences or publishing a paper (Pakistan R2).

Students complained about not enough staffs in this department (Iran R2, China R1), if there were enough staffs in this department to answer to students requests was better because sometimes you must be wait for more than one hour to asking a question (China R1).most of the time there is just one staff in graduate school and she must answer to all requests, its natural that if you want to reach your request you must wait for more than one hour (China R1).

Students need more medical facilities in health centre (Iran R2, Indonesia R 1), they also request for having specialist doctors in this department and using more effective medicine (Iraq R2, Indonesia R2, Nigeria R 2, Iran R1), according to one of the Iraqis students most of the times the medicine which supposed by the doctors is not suitable to the disease. I don't know why but the health centre doctors have strong interest to give pain killer to patients even as time as the patient don't have any pain or the disease is not related to pain killer (Nigeria R2).

Its obviously that more respondents are needed to verify the allegation of these respondent.

4.1.2 Interview summary

The interview results show that Most of the foreign students are unsatisfied about the recreational facilities and programs furthermore most of them are faced with financial problems they complain that the University don't have enough on campus recreational facility and equipment. on the other hand the foreign students are faced with financial problems because most of them don't receive any financial support from their family or government and regarding to this problem they faced difficulty about submitting their papers in journals and conferences because most of the lecturers prefer to support local students instead of foreigners specially in this case. Finally all the participates suggest that it will be good for University to consider a complain/suggestion box in each department, office faculties and hostels.

It will be a good opportunity to all students to voice out their suggestions and complaints.

4.2 Analyses of quantitative report

In this part analyzed the questioners collected back from the foreign postgraduate students in target University. Statistical package for social sciences (SPSS) version 15.0 for windows was used in this research to analyze the data gathering. Firstly demographics of sample followed by foreign postgraduate students, secondly the frequency and percentages of the foreign students problems in eleven categories and lastly the most highest items of foreign postgraduate students problems in each category of problems separated by their gender and country of origins will analyzed.

- Analysis of demographic data

- Analysis of the most disturbing category

- Analysis of the most disturbing items

4.2.1 Analysis of Respondents background

The demographics of respondents will be discussed in this part which is consists of gender, country of origins, marital status and semester of the study.

4.2.2 Respondents gender

Table 4.1 Represents the frequency and percentages of the respondents according to their gender, regarding to the table out of 430 respondents, there were 257 male respondents, which represented 59.8 % .on the other hand female respondents, have 173 persons (40.2 %).

Table 4.2 Distribution of respondents according to gender

No	Gender	Percentage
1	Male	62.7
2	Female	37.3
3	Total	100%

4.2.3 Respondents country of origins

Table 4.2 indicates the distribution of respondents according to age, all the respondents' country of origins. As you can see, most of the respondent's populations are come from Iran 221 person around 62.4%,other respondents frequency and percentages respectively are include: Indonesia 43 persons (12.1 %) , Nigeria 30 persons (8.5%), Iraq 30 persons (8.5%), Pakistan 30 persons (8.5%).

4.2.4 Respondents marital status

Table 4.3 Distribution of respondents according to the country of origin

No	Country of origin	Percentage
1	Iran	62.4
2	Indonesia	12.1
3	Nigeria	8.5
4	Iraq	8.5
5	Pakistan	8.5
6	Total	100

Table 4.3 indicates the frequency and percentage of the respondents according to their marital status, out of 354 respondents, 259 persons (83.3%) are single and 59 persons (16.7%) are married.

Table 4.4 Distribution of respondents according to the marital status

No	Marital status	Percentage
1	Single	83.3
2	Married	16.7
3	Total	100

4.2.5 Respondents semester of study

Table 4.5 Percentage of the respondents according to their semester of study

No	Semester of study	Percentage
1	First semester	24 %
2	Second semester	37%
3	Third semester	33.3%

4.2.6 Analysis of the most disturbing category of problems

Table 4.6 Percentage in each category of problems based on respondents yes answered

No	Categories	Percentage
1	Social and recreational problems	17%
2	Financial, lifestyle and career related problems	11%
3	Curriculum and method of teaching problems	11%
4	Personal relationships and emotional problems	10%
5	Marriage and sexual problems	10%
6	Future career adapting problems	10%
7	Adapting to academic work problems	9%
8	Psychological social relation problems	7%
9	Health related problems	5%
10	Family problems	5%
11	Moral and religious problems	5%

Table 4.6 indicates the percentages of the yes answered by the respondents in each category of problems. As the table show respondents give the most yes answered to category number three (social and recreational problems) around (17 %) and the other category percentages respectively are include: category number 2 (financial, lifestyle and career related problems) 11%, category number 11 (curriculum and method of teaching problems) 11%, category number 5 (personal relationships and emotional problems) 10% , category number 6 (marriage and sexual problems) 10%, category number 10 (future career adapting problems) 10%, category number 9 (adapting to academic work problems) 9%, category number 4 (psychological social relation problems) 7%, category number 1 (health related problems) 5%,

category number 7 (family problems) 5% and category number 8 (moral and religious problems) 5%.

4.2.7 Percentage of the most disturbing items in each category of problems

Table 4.7 Most disturbing items in Health relate problems

No	Items	Percentage
1	Lack of exercise	54.5
2	Easily tired out	44.6
3	Need medical advise	31.9
4	Lack of sleep	31.4
5	Easily stressed out and headache	26.8

This table shows lack of exercise 54.4%, easily tired out 44.6%, need medical advice 31.9%, lack of sleep 31.4% and easily stressed out and headache 26.8%.

Table 4.8 Most disturbing items in financial, lifestyle and career related problems

No	Items	Percentage
1	Bored of the same food	61.6
2	Working is for my own benefit	58.2
3	Need of part-time job	57.9
4	Not sure of future allowance	51.4
5	In need of job during holiday	49.4

This table shows , bored of the same food 61.6%, working is for my own benefit 58.2%, need of part-time job 57.9%, not sure of future allowance 51.4% and In need of job during holiday 49.4%.

Table 4.9 Most disturbing items in social and recreational problems

No	Items	Percentage
1	Willing to improve my thoughts	82.5
2	Interested in vacations	81.1
3	Need more opportunity to express myself	72
4	Interested in entertaining	71.5
5	Interested in improving ethics	67.8

This table shows, willing to improve my thoughts 82.5%, interested in vacations 81.1%, need more opportunity to express myself 72%, interested in entertaining 71.5% and interested in improving ethics 67.8%

Table 4.10 Percentage of the most disturbing items in psychological social relation problems

No	Items	Percentage
1	Missing someone at home	73.4
2	Interested in a better personality	72.3
3	Avoid oneself from those that you hate	28.8
4	Easily embarrassed	26.8
5	Acting without thinking	26.3

This table shows, missing someone at home 73.4%, interested in a better personality 72.3%, avoid oneself from those that you hate 28.8%, easily embarrassed 26.8% and acting without thinking 26.3%.

Table 4.11 Percentage of the most disturbing items in personal relationships and emotional problems

No	Item	Percentage
1	Thinking seriously about something	74.3
2	Being easily happy	62.1
3	Feels that life is not perfect	49.4
4	Afraid of mistakes	47.7
5	Unable to forget bad experiences	41.8

This table shows, thinking seriously about something 74.3%, being easily happy 62.1%, feels that life is not perfect 49.4%, afraid of mistakes 47.7% and unable to forget bad experiences 41.8%.

Table 4.12 Percentage of the most disturbing items in marriage and sexual problems

No	Items	Percentage
1	Thinking about finding the right person	56.5
2	Thinking of the future prospect person	54
3	Thinking if the marriage will succeed	53.1
4	Afraid of losing the one you love	44.1
5	Shy to talk about sex	44.1

This table shows, thinking about finding the right person 56.5%, thinking of the future prospect person 54%, thinking if the marriage will succeed 53.1%, afraid of losing the one you love 44.1% and shy to talk about sex 44.1%.

Table 4.13 Percentage of the most disturbing items in family problems

No	Items	Percentage
1	Parents have high expectations	50
2	Worried about a particular person in the family	46.3
3	Having a huge responsibility	46.3
4	Rarely going back home	42.7
5	In need of love and care	39.8

This table shows, parents have high expectations 50%, worried about a particular person in the family 46.3%, having a huge responsibility 46.3%, rarely going back home 42.7% and In need of love and care 39.8%.

Table 4.14 Percentage of the most disturbing items in moral and religious problems

No	Item	Percentage
1	Interested in getting to know God	60.7
2	Rarely visit the temple/church/mosque	48.6
3	Need of principles in life	46.6
4	Remembering the mistakes committed	40.4
5	Need more opportunities of religion	35.6

This table shows, interested in getting to know god 60.7%, rarely visit the temple/church/mosque 48.6%, need of principles in life 46.6%, remembering the mistakes committed 40.4% and need more opportunities of religion 35.6%.

Table 4.15 Percentage of the most disturbing items in adapting to academic work problems

No	Item	Percentage
1	Easily disturbed while doing a work	40.1
2	Forgotten those learned before	38.7
3	Unable to focus well	36.2
4	Afraid of failing	34.5
5	Need a break from school	33.6

This table shows easily disturbed while doing a work 40.1%, forgotten those learned before 38.7%, unable to focus well 36.2%, afraid of failing 34.5% and need a break from school 33.6%.

Table 4.16 Percentage of the most disturbing items in career adapting problems

No	Item	Percentage
1	Need of planning for the future	67.8
2	Need of information about career	66.7
3	Need of ability to work	60.2
4	Need of decision about career	57.1
5	Choosing a good course for a good career	54.5

This table shows need of planning for the future 67.8%, need of information about career 66.7%, need of ability to work 60.2%, need of decision about career 57.1% and choosing a good course for a good career 54.5%.

Table 4.17 Percentage of the most disturbing items in curriculum and method of teaching problems

No	Items	Percentage
1	Boring classes	49.4
2	Lots of work and assignments	46.6
3	Lecturers are too theoretical	43.8
4	College is not concerned of students needs	43.2
5	Lecturers are inefficient in teaching a certain subject	42.9

This table shows boring classes 49.4%, lots of work and assignments 46.6%, lecturers are too theoretical 43.8%, college is not concerned of students' needs 43.2% and lecturers are inefficient in teaching a certain subject 42.9%.

4.2.8 Analyse of the most disturbing items in each category of problems in term of respondents' gender

Tables 4.18 Percentage of the most disturbing items among foreign male and female and male students in Health related problems

No	Items	Female
		Percentage
1	Lack of exercise	67.4
2	Easily tired out	55.3
3	Need medical advise	40.9
4	Easily stressed out and headache	34.8
5	Lack of exercise	67.4

No	Items	Male
		Percentage
1	Lack of exercise	46.8
2	Easily tired out	38.3
3	Lack of sleep	30.6
4	Need medical advise	26.6
5	Allergy (fever, asthma rashes and others)	24.3

This tables shows menstruation problem lack of exercise 67.4 %, easily tired out 55.3 %, need medical advise 40.9 %, easily stressed out and headache 34.8% among females in health related problems and lack of exercise 46.8%, easily tired out 38.3%, lack of sleep 30.6%, need medical advise 26.6%, allergy (fever, asthma rashes and others) 24.3% among Males .

Tables 4.19 Percentage of the most disturbing items among foreign female and male students in financial, lifestyle and career related problems

No	Items	Female
		Percentage
1	Need of part-time job	58.3
2	Working is for my own benefit	58.3
3	Transportation problem	56.9
4	Bored of the same food	56.9
5	Need to control usage of money	56.1

No	Items	Male
		Percentage
1	Bored of the same food	64.4
2	Working is for my own benefit	58.5
3	Need of part-time job	57.6
4	Not sure of future allowance	51.8
5	In need of job during holiday	50.4

This tables indicates need of part-time job 58.3%, working is for my own benefit 58.3%, transportation problem 56.9%, bored of the same food 56.9 %, need to control usage of money 56.1% among females and bored of the same food 64.4%, working is for my own benefit 58.5%, need of part-time job 57.6%, not sure of future allowance 51.8%, In need of job during holiday 50.4% among male students.

Tables 4.20 Percentage of the most disturbing items among foreign
female and males students in Social and recreational problems

No	Items	Female Percentage
1	Willing to improve my thoughts	90.9
2	Need more opportunity to express myself	72.3
3	Interested in improving ethics	71.2
4	Interested in entertaining	66.7
5	Interested in changing appearance	61.4

No	Items	Male Percentage
1	Interested in vacations	80.1
2	Willing to improve my thoughts	77.5
3	Interested in entertaining	74.3
4	Interested in improving ethics	70.3
5	Need more opportunity to express myself	68.9

This tables represents willing to improve my thoughts 90.9 %,
need more opportunity to express myself 72.3 %, interested in improving
ethics 71.2 %, interested in entertaining 66.7%, interested in changing
appearance 61.4% among females and interested in vacations 80.1%,
willing to improve my thoughts 77.5%, Interested in entertaining 74.3%,
interested in improving ethics 70.3%, need more opportunity to express
myself 68.9% among males.

Tables 4.21 Percentage of the most disturbing items among foreign female and male students in Psychological social relation problems

No	Items	Female
		Percentage
1	Interested in a better personality	81.1
2	Missing someone at home	78.8
3	Easily embarrassed	33.3
4	Difficulty in expressing oneself	31.9
5	Feeling lost	29.5

No	Items	Male
		Percentage
1	Missing someone at home	70.3
2	Interested in a better personality	67.1
3	Avoid oneself from those that you hate	28.8
4	Easily influenced by others	25.7
5	Worried about being nice to others	25.2

This tables shows, interested in a better personality 81.1%, missing someone at home 78.8%, easily embarrassed 33.3%, difficulty in expressing oneself 31.9%, feeling lost 29.5% among females and missing someone at home 70.3%, interested in a better personality 67.1%, avoid oneself from those that you hate 28.8%, easily influenced by others 25.7%, worried about being nice to others 25.2% among males.

Table's 4.22 Percentage of the most disturbing items among foreign female and male students in Personal relationships and emotional problems

No	Items	Female
		Percentage
1	Thinking seriously about something	81.1
2	Being easily happy	69
3	Afraid of mistakes	56.9
4	Being worried unnecessarily	54.5
5	Feels that life is not perfect	52.3

No	Items	Male
		Percentage
1	Thinking seriously about something	70.3
2	Being easily happy	58.1
3	Feels that life is not perfect	47.7
4	Afraid of mistakes	42.3
5	Unable to forget bad experiences	38.3

These tables shows, thinking seriously about something 81.1 %, being easily happy 69%, afraid of mistakes 56.9%, being worried unnecessarily 54.5%, feels that life is not perfect 52.3 % among females and thinking seriously about something 70.35, being easily happy 58.1%, feels that life is not perfect 47.7%, afraid of mistakes 42.3%, unable to forget bad experiences 38.3% among males.

Tables 4.23 Percentage of the most disturbing items among foreign female and males students in Marriage and sexual problems

No	Items	Female
		Percentage
1	Thinking about finding the right person	65.9
2	Afraid of losing the one you love	61.4
3	Thinking of the future prospect person	59.8
4	Thinking if the marriage will succeed	59.8
5	Shy to talk about sex	56.9

No	Items	Male
		Percentage
1	Thinking about finding the right person	50.9
2	Thinking of the future prospect person	50.4
3	Thinking if the marriage will succeed	49.1
4	Taking decision to maintain a relationship	43.7
5	Being in love	42.3

This tables illustrates, thinking about finding the right person 65.9 %, afraid of losing the one you love 61.4%, thinking of the future prospect person 59.8%, thinking if the marriage will succeed 59.8%, shy to talk about sex 56.9% among females and thinking about finding the right person 50.9%, thinking of the future prospect person 50.4%, thinking if the marriage will succeed 49.1%, taking decision to maintain a relationship 43.7%, and being in love 42.3% among males.

Tables 4.24 Analyse percentage of the most disturbing items among foreign female and males students in Family problems

No	Items	Female
		Percentage
1	Parents have high expectations	65.1
2	Worried about a particular person in the family	56.1
3	Having a huge responsibility	52.3
4	In need of love and care	52.3
5	Do not share everything with parents	44.1

No	Items	Male
		Percentage
1	Having a huge responsibility	42.8
2	Rarely going back home	41.9
3	Parents have high expectations	41
4	Worried about a particular person in the family	40.5
5	Do not share everything with parents	33.3

This tables shows, parents have high expectations 65.1%, worried about a particular person in the family 56.1%, having a huge responsibility 52.3 %, in need of love and care 52.3%, do not share everything with parents 44.1% among females and having a huge responsibility 42.8%, rarely going back home 41.9%, Parents have high expectations 41%, worried about a particular person in the family 40.5%, do not share everything with parents 33.3% among males.

Tables 4.25 Percentage of the most disturbing items among foreign female and males students in Moral and religious problems

No	Items	Female
		Percentage
1	Interested in getting to know God	56.9
2	Rarely visit the temple	52.3
3	Need of principles in life	48.5
4	Interested in understanding the bible/Guran/engil	40.2
5	Remembering the mistakes committed	34.8

No	Items	Male
		Percentage
1	Interested in getting to know God	63.1
2	Rarely visit the temple/Mosque/Church	46.4
3	Need of principles in life	45.5
4	Remembering the mistakes committed	43.7
5	Need more opportunities of religion	36.5

This tables represents, interested in getting to know god 56.9%, Rarely visit the temple 52.3%, need of principles in life 48.5%, interested in understanding the bible/Ghoran/engil 40.2%, remembering the mistakes committed 34.8% among females and interested in getting to know God 63.1%, rarely visit the temple 46.4%, need of principles in life 45.5%, remembering the mistakes committed 43.7%, need more opportunities of religion 36.5% among males.

Tables 4.26 Percentage of the most disturbing items among foreign female students in Adapting to academic work problems

No	Items	Female
		Percentage
1	Easily disturbed while doing a work	47
2	Forgotten those learned before	46
3	Unable to focus well	46
4	Worried of exams	44.1
5	Poor vocabulary	40.9

No	Items	Percentage
1	Easily disturbed while doing a work	36
2	Forgotten those learned before	34.2
3	Need a break from school	33.3
4	Afraid of failing	31.5
5	Unable to focus well	30.2

This tables shows easily disturbed while doing a work 47%, forgotten those learned before 46%, unable to focus well 46%, worried of exams 44.1%, poor vocabulary 40.9% among females and easily disturbed while doing a work 36%, forgotten those learned before 34.2%, need a break from school 33.3%, afraid of failing 31.5%, unable to focus well 30.2% among males.

Tables 4.27 Percentage of the most disturbing items among foreign female and males students in Future career adapting problems

No	Items	Female Percentage
1	Need of information about career	78.7
2	Need of planning for the future	75.7
3	Need of decision about career	72.7
4	Choosing a good course for a good career	65.1
5	Need of ability to work	64.4

No	Items	Male Percentage
1	Need of planning for the future	63.1
2	Need of information about career	59.5
3	Need of ability to work	57.2
4	Choosing a good course for a good career	48.2
5	Need of earlier experience	47.7

This tables indicates, need of information about career 78.7%, need of planning for the future 75.7%, need of decision about career 72.7%, choosing a good course for a good career 65.1% and need of ability to work 64.4% among females and need of planning for the future 63.1%, need of information about career 59.5%, need of ability to work 57.2%, choosing a good course for a good career 48.2%, need of earlier experience 47.7% among males.

Tables 4.28 Percentage of the most disturbing items among foreign female and males students in Curriculum and method of teaching problems

No	Items	Female
		Percentage
1	Lots of work and assignments	57.6
2	Boring classes	52.3
3	Lecturers are too theoretical	50
4	Too many rules and regulations	48.5
5	Lack of a good college advisor	43.9

No	Items	Male
		Percentage
1	Boring classes	47.7
2	Lecturers are inefficient in teaching a certain subject	45
3	College is not concerned of students needs	43.2
4	Less lively campus	42.3
5	Lack of a good college advisor	41.4

This tables shows, lots of work and assignments 57.6%, boring classes 52.3%, lecturers are too theoretical 50%, too many rules and regulations 48.5 %, lack of a good college advisor 43.9 % among females and boring classes 47.7%, lecturers are inefficient in teaching a certain subject 45%; college is not concerned of students' needs 43.2%, less lively campus 42.3%, lack of a good college advisor 41.4% among males.

4.2.9 Analyse the most disturbing items in each category of problems in term of respondents' country of origin

Table 4.29 Percentage of the most disturbing items among Iranian students in Health related problems

No	Items	Iran
		Percentage
1	Lack of exercise	60.6
2	Easily tired out	57.9
3	Lack of sleep	38
4	Easily stressed out and headache	30.3
5	Need medical advise	29.9

This table shows lack of exercise 60.6%, easily tired out 57.9%, lack of sleep 38%, easily stressed out and headache 30.3%, need medical advice 29.9%.

Table 4.30 Percentage of the most disturbing items among Iranian students in Financial, lifestyle and career related problems

No	Items	Iran Percentage
1	Need of part-time job	62
2	Working is for my own benefit	61.5
3	Bored of the same food	59.7
4	Not sure of future allowance	52.9
5	Dislike financial support from others	49.8

This table shows need of part-time job 62%, working is for my own benefit 61.2%, Bored of the same food 59.7%, not sure of future allowance 52.9%, dislike financial support from others 49.8%.

Table 4.31 Percentage of the most disturbing items among Iranian students in Social and recreational problems

No	Items	Iran Percentage
1	Interested in vacations	85.5
2	Willing to improve my thoughts	80.1
3	Interested in improving ethics	70.6
4	Need more opportunity to express myself	67
5	Interested in changing appearance	63.3

This table shows Interested in vacations 85.5%, Willing to improve my thoughts 80.5%, Interested in improving ethics 70.6%, Need more opportunity to express myself 67%, Interested in changing appearance 63.3%.

Table 4.32 Percentage of the most disturbing items among Iranian students in Psychological social relation problems

No	Items	Iran
		Percentage
1	Missing someone at home	73.7
2	Feeling uncomfortable with others	72.4
3	Easily hurt others feelings	32.1
4	Ill-talked about	27.6
5	Avoid oneself from those that you hate	24.9

This table shows missing someone at home 73.7%, feeling uncomfortable with others 72.4%, easily hurt others feelings 32.1%, Ill-talked about 27.6%, avoid oneself from those that you hate 24.9%.

Table 4.33 Percentage of the most disturbing items among Iranian students in Personal relationships and emotional problems

No	Items	Iran
		Percentage
1	Thinking seriously about something	72.8
2	Being easily happy	56.6
3	Feels that life is not perfect	51.6
4	Afraid of mistakes	49.8
5	Unable to forget bad experiences	43.9

This table shows Thinking seriously about something 72.8%, Being easily happy 56.6%, Feels that life is not perfect 51.6%, Afraid of mistakes 49.8%, Unable to forget bad experiences 43.9%.

Table 4.34 Percentage of the most disturbing items among Iranian students in Marriage and sexual problems

No	Items	Iran Percentage
1	Thinking about finding the right person	61.5
2	Thinking of the future prospect person	59.3
3	Thinking if the marriage will succeed	58
4	Love failure	57.9
5	Shy to talk about sex	46.6

This table shows thinking about finding the right person 61.5%, thinking of the future prospect person 59.3%, thinking if the marriage will succeed 58%, thinking if the marriage will succeed 57.9%, shy to talk about sex 46.6%.

Table 4.35 Percentage of the most disturbing items among Iranian students in Family problems

No	Items	Iran Percentage
1	Parents have high expectations	52
2	Worried about a particular person in the family	49.8
3	Rarely going back home	41.6
4	Do not share everything with parents	41.2
5	Having a huge responsibility	40.3

This table shows Parents have high expectations 52%, Worried about a particular person in the family 49.8%, Rarely going back home 41.6%, Do not share everything with parents 41.2%, Having a huge responsibility 40.3%.

Table 4.36 Percentage of the most disturbing items among Iranian students in Moral and religious problems

No	Items	Iran
		Percentage
1	Interested in getting to know God	56.6
2	Rarely visit the temple	46.1
3	Need of principles in life	29.4
4	Remembering the mistakes committed	35.3
5	Interested in understanding the bible	58.8

This table shows interested in getting to know God 56.6% rarely visit the temple 46.1%, need of principles in life 29.4%, remembering the mistakes committed 35.3%, interested in understanding the bible 58.8%.

Table 4.37 Percentage of the most disturbing items among Iranian students in Adapting to academic work problems

No	Items	Iran
		Percentage
1	Unable to focus well	43.9
2	Easily disturbed while doing a work	39.8
3	Forgotten those learned before	39.8
4	Afraid of failing	36.6
5	Weak in writing skills	35.3

This table shows unable to focus well 43.9%, easily disturbed while doing a work 39.8%, forgotten those learned before 39.8%, afraid of failing 36.6%, weak in writing skills 35.3%.

Table 4.38 Percentages of the most disturbing items among Iranian
students in Future career adapting problems

No	Items	Iran
		Percentage
1	Need of information about career	70.6
2	Need of planning for the future	68.3
3	Need of ability to work	57.9
4	Need of advice while preparing for college or university	57.7
5	Need of decision about career	57

This table shows need of information about career 70.35, need of
planning for the future 68.3, need of ability to work 57.9%, need of
advice while preparing for college or university 57.7%, need of decision
about career 57%.

Table 4.39 Percentage of the most disturbing items among Iranian
students in Curriculum and method of teaching problems

No	Items	Iran
		Percentage
1	Boring classes	56.6
2	Lack of a good college advisor	51.6
3	Lecturers are inefficient in teaching a certain subject	50.2
4	Lots of work and assignments	48
5	Lecturers are too theoretical	45.7

This table shows boring classes 56.6%, lack of a good college
advisor 51.6%, lecturers are inefficient in teaching a certain subject
50.2%, lots of work and assignments 48%, lecturers are too theoretical
45.7%.

Table 4.40 Percentage of the most disturbing items among Indonesian students in Health related problems

No	Items	Indonesia Percentage
1	Lack of exercise	39.5
2	Often having flu	39.5
3	Easily tired out	37.2
4	Digestion problem	30.2
5	Dental problem	25.6

This table shows lack of exercise 39.5%, often having flu 39.5%, easily tired out 37.2%, digestion problem 30.2%, dental problem 25.6%.

Table 4.41 Percentage of the most disturbing items among Indonesian students in Financial, lifestyle and career related problems

No	Items	Indonesia Percentage
1	Bored of the same food	79.1
2	Need to control usage of money	65.1
3	Need of part-time job	62.8
4	Working is for my own benefit	62.8
5	In need of job during holiday	58.1

This table shows bored of the same food 79.1%, need to control usage of money 65.1%, need of part-time job 62.8%, working is for my own benefit 62.8%, in need of job during holiday 58.1%.

Table 4.42 Percentage of the most disturbing items among Indonesian students in Social and recreational problems

No	Items	Indonesia
		Percentage
1	Need more opportunity to express myself	95.3
2	Willing to improve my thoughts	93
3	Interested in vacations	88.4
4	Lack of recreations	72.1
5	Interested in more discussions	72.1

This table shows need more opportunity to express myself 95.3%, willing to improve my thoughts 93%, interested in vacations 88.4%, lack of recreations 72.1%, interested in more discussions 72.1%.

Table 4.43 Percentage of the most disturbing items among Indonesian students in Psychological social relation problems

No	Items	Indonesia
		Percentage
1	Missing someone at home	72.1
2	Interested in a better personality	72.1
3	Easily embarrassed	44.2
4	Easily influenced by others	32.6
5	Lack of leadership skills	32.6

This table shows missing someone at home 72.1%, interested in a better personality 72.1%, easily embarrassed 44.2%, easily influenced by others 32.6%, lack of leadership skills 32.6%.

Table 4.44 Percentage of the most disturbing items among Indonesian students in Personal relationships and emotional problems

No	Items	Indonesia
		Percentage
1	Thinking seriously about something	93
2	Being easily happy	76.7
3	Feels that life is not perfect	51.2
4	Being worried unnecessarily	48.8
5	Lack of confidence	47.9

This table shows thinking seriously about something 93%, being easily happy 76.7%, feels that life is not perfect 51.2%, being worried unnecessarily 48.8%, lack of confidence 47.9%.

Table 4.45 Percentage of the most disturbing items among Indonesian students in Marriage and sexual problems

No	Items	Indonesia
		Percentage
1	Thinking if the marriage will succeed	69.8
2	Thinking of the future prospect person	65.1
3	Thinking about finding the right person	62.8
4	Being in love	60.5
5	Thinking if I will ever get married	53.5

This table shows thinking if the marriage will succeed 69.8%, thinking of the future prospect person 65.1%, thinking about finding the right person 62.8%, being in love 60.5%, thinking if I will ever get married 53.3%.

Table 4.46 Percentage of the most disturbing items among Indonesian students in Family problems

No	Items	Indonesia Percentage
1	Having a huge responsibility	72
2	Parents have high expectations	58.1
3	In need of love and care	53.5
4	Rarely going back home	53.5
5	Worried about a particular person in the family	37.2

This table shows having a huge responsibility 72%, parents have high expectations 58.1%, in need of love and care 53.3%, rarely going back home 53.3%, worried about a particular person in the family 37.2%.

Table 4.47 Percentage of the most disturbing items among Indonesian students in Moral and religious problems

No	Items	Indonesia Percentage
1	Need of principles in life	72.1
2	Interested in getting to know God	72.1
3	Need more opportunities of religion	60.5
4	Rarely visit the temple	34.9
5	Feeling guilty	27.9

This table shows need of principles in life 72.1%, interested in getting to know God 72.1%, need more opportunities of religion 60.5%, rarely visit the temple 34.9%, feeling guilty 27.9%.

Table 4.48 Percentage of the most disturbing items among Indonesian students in Adapting to academic work problems

No	Items	Indonesia
		Percentage
1	Easily disturbed while doing a work	67.4
2	Forgotten those learned before	51.2
3	Lack of exercise while in high school	46.5
4	Unable to focus well	44.2
5	Weak in writing skills	37.2

This table shows easily disturbed while doing a work 67.4%, forgotten those learned before 51.2%, lack of exercise while in high school 46.5%, unable to focus well 44.2%, weak in writing skills 37.2%.

Table 4.49 Percentages of the most disturbing items among Indonesian students in Future career adapting problems

No	Items	Indonesia
		Percentage
1	Need of ability to work	88.4
2	Need of planning for the future	86
3	Need of information about career	79.1
4	Need of earlier experience	74.4
5	Need of decision about career	74.4

This table shows Need of ability to work 88.4%, Need of planning for the future 86%, Need of information about career 79.1%, Need of earlier experience 74.4%, Need of decision about career 74.4%.

Table 4.50 Percentage of the most disturbing items among Indonesian students in Curriculum and method of teaching problems

No	Items	Indonesia Percentage
1	College is not concerned of students needs	46.5
2	Campus is lack of recreational facilities	46.5
3	Poor arrangement of campus activities	41.9
4	Too many rules and regulations	37.2
5	Unable to get required books	34.9

This table shows college is not concerned of students needs 46.5%, campus is lack of recreational facilities 46.5%, poor arrangement of campus activities 41.9%, too many rules and regulations 37.2%, unable to get required books 34.9%.

Table 4.51 Percentage of the most disturbing items among Nigerian students in health related problems

No	Items	Nigeria Percentage
1	Lack of exercise	53.3
2	Need medical advise	46.7
3	Allergy (fever, asthma rashes and others)	36.7
4	Digestion problem	33.3
5	Easily tired out	26.7

This table shows lack of exercise 53.3%, need medical advise 46.7%, allergy (fever, asthma rashes and others) 36.7%, digestion problem 33.3%, easily tired out 26.7%.

Table 4.52 Percentage of the most disturbing items among Nigerian students in Financial, lifestyle and career related problems

No	Items	Nigeria Percentage
1	Working till late at night	53.3
2	Bored of the same food	53.3
3	Need of part-time job	46.7
4	In need of job during holiday	46.7
5	Working is for my own benefit	46.7

This table shows working till late at night 53.3%, bored of the same food 53.3%, need of part-time job 46.7%, in need of job during holiday 46.7%, working is for my own benefit 46.7%.

Table 4.53 Percentage of the most disturbing items among Nigerian students in Social and recreational problems

No	Items	Nigeria Percentage
1	Interested in vacations	86.7
2	Interested in improving ethics	73.3
3	No enjoyment during holidays	73.3
4	Lack of opportunities for entertainment	66.7
5	Willing to improve my thoughts	66.7

This table shows interested in vacations 86.7%, interested in improving ethics 73.3%, no enjoyment during holidays 73.3%, lack of opportunities for entertainment 66.7%, willing to improve my thoughts 66.7%.

Table 4.54 Percentage of the most disturbing items among Nigerian students in Psychological social relation problems

No	Items	Nigeria Percentage
1	Missing someone at home	83.3
2	Interested in a better personality	80
3	Feeling lost	36.7
4	Lacking behind in most things	30
5	Acting without thinking	30

This table shows missing someone at home 83.3%, interested in a better personality 80%, feeling lost 36.7%, lacking behind in most things 30%, acting without thinking 30%.

Table 4.55 Percentage of the most disturbing items among Nigerian students in Personal relationships and emotional problems

No	Items	Nigeria Percentage
1	Being easily happy	73.3
2	Thinking seriously about something	70
3	Feels that life is not perfect	66.7
4	Lazy	36.7
5	Being worried unnecessarily	33.3

This table shows being easily happy 73.3%, thinking seriously about something 70%, feels that life is not perfect 66.7%, lazy 36.7%, being worried unnecessarily 33.3%.

Table 4.56 Percentage of the most disturbing items among Nigerian students in Marriage and sexual problems

No	Items	Nigeria
		Percentage
1	Too strict in sex related issues	56.7
2	Shy to talk about sex	53.3
3	Taking decision to maintain a relationship	50
4	Afraid of losing the one you love	46.7
5	Being in love	46.7

This table shows too strict in sex related issues 56.7%, shy to talk about sex 53.3%, taking decision to maintain a relationship 50%, afraid of losing the one you love 46.7%, being in love 46.7%.

Table 4.57 Percentage of the most disturbing items among Nigerian students in Family problems

No	Items	Nigeria
		Percentage
1	Having a huge responsibility	56.7
2	In need of love and care	46.7
3	Parents struggle for me	45.3
4	Worried about a particular person in the family	40
5	Cannot discuss about a problem at home	30

This table shows having a huge responsibility 56.7%, in need of love and care 46.7%, parents struggle for me 45.3%, worried about a particular person in the family 40%, cannot discuss about a problem at home 30%.

Table 4.58 Percentage of the most disturbing items among Nigerian students in Moral and religious problems

No	Items	Nigeria Percentage
1	Interested in getting to know God	83.3
2	Need more opportunities of religion	56.7
3	Rarely visit the temple/church/mosque	50
4	Need of principles in life	40
5	Pretending	33.3

This table shows interested in getting to know God 83.3%, need more opportunities of religion 56.7%, rarely visit the temple 50%, need of principles in life 40%, pretending 33.3%.

Table 4.59 Percentage of the most disturbing items among Nigerian students in Adapting to academic work problems

No	Items	Nigeria Percentage
1	Need a break from school	60
2	Lack of time for studies	26.7
3	Worried of exams	26.7
4	Afraid of failing	26.7
5	Forgotten those learned before	20

This table shows need a break from school 60%, lack of time for studies 26.7%, worried of exams 26.7%, afraid of failing 26.7%, forgotten those learned before 20%.

Table 4.60 Percentages of the most disturbing items among Nigerian students in Future career adapting problems

No	Items	Nigeria Percentage
1	Trying to combine marriage and career	50
2	Need of ability to work	50
3	Choosing a good course for a good career	50
4	Need of planning for the future	46.7
5	Need of information about career	46.7

This table shows Trying to combine marriage and career 50%, need of ability to work 50%, choosing a good course for a good career 50%, need of planning for the future 46.7%, need of information about career 46.7%.

Table 4.61 Percentage of the most disturbing items among Nigerian students in Curriculum and method of teaching problems

No	Items	Nigeria Percentage
1	Lots of work and assignments	63.3
2	Less lively campus	50
3	Lack of discussion in class	36.7
4	Classes are as those in high schools	36.7
5	Teaching is inefficient	36.7

This table shows lots of work and assignments 63.3%, less lively campus 50%, lack of discussion in class 36.7%, classes are as those in high schools 36.7%, teaching is inefficient 36.7%.

Table 4.62 Percentage of the most disturbing items among Iraq students in Health related problems

No	Items	Iraq Percentage
1	Lack of sleep	40
2	Lack of exercise	36.7
3	Need medical advise	36.7
4	Frequent headache	30
5	Easily stressed out and headache	20

This table shows lack of sleep 40%, lack of exercise 36.7%, need medical advise 36.7%, frequent headache 30%, easily stressed out and headache 20%.

Table 4.63 Percentage of the most disturbing items among Iraq students in Financial, lifestyle and career related problems

No	Items	Iraq Percentage
1	Bored of the same food	56.7
2	In need of job during holiday	50
3	Need of part-time job	43.3
4	No entertainment with friends	40
5	No satisfaction and diet	36.7

This table shows bored of the same food 56.7%, in need of job during holiday 50%, need of part-time job 43.3%, no entertainment with friends 40%, no satisfaction and diet 36.7%.

Table 4.64 Percentage of the most disturbing items among Iraq students in Social and recreational problems

No	Items	Iraq Percentage
1	Willing to improve my thoughts	86.7
2	Interested in vacations	70
3	Need more opportunity to express myself	66.7
4	Lack of time for art and music	60
5	Lack of opportunities for entertainment	60

This table shows willing to improve my thoughts 86.7%, interested in vacations 70%, need more opportunity to express myself 66.7%, lack of time for art and music 60%, lack of opportunities for entertainment 60%.

Table 4.65 Percentage of the most disturbing items among Iraq students in Psychological social relation problems

No	Items	Iraq Percentage
1	Missing someone at home	66.7
2	Interested in a better personality	56.7
3	Jealous	36.7
4	Being hated by someone	33.3
5	Worried how I captivate other people	30

This table shows missing someone at home 66.7%, interested in a better personality 56.7%, Jealous 36.7%, being hated by someone 33.3%, worried how I captivate other people 30%.

Table 4.66 Percentage of the most disturbing items among Iraq students
in Personal relationships and emotional problems

No	Items	Iraq Percentage
1	Thinking seriously about something	63.3
2	Being easily happy	53.3
3	Afraid of mistakes	50
4	Forgetful	46.7
5	Being worried unnecessarily	30

This table shows thinking seriously about something 63.3%, being easily happy 53.3%, afraid of mistakes 50%, forgetful 46.7%, being worried unnecessarily 30%.

Table 4.67 Percentage of the most disturbing items among Iraq students
in Marriage and sexual problems

No	Items	Iraq Percentage
1	Afraid of losing the one you love	40
2	Thinking about finding the right person	36.7
3	Thinking if the marriage will succeed	36.7
4	Being in love	30
5	Thinking of the future prospect person	30

This table shows afraid of losing the one you love 40%, thinking about finding the right person 36.7%, thinking if the marriage will succeed 36.7%, being in love 30%, thinking of the future prospect person 30%.

Table 4.68 Percentage of the most disturbing items among Iraq students in Family problems

No	Items	Iraq Percentage
1	Parents have high expectations	46.7
2	Having a huge responsibility	46.7
3	Do not share everything with parents	46.7
4	Worried about a particular person in the family	36.7
5	Parents struggle for me	33.3

This table shows Parents have high expectations 46.7%, Having a huge responsibility 46.7%, Do not share everything with parents 46.7%, Worried about a particular person in the family 36.7%, Parents struggle for me 33.3%.

Table 4.69 Percentage of the most disturbing items among Iraq students in Moral and religious problems

No	Items	Iraq Percentage
1	Interested in getting to know God	46.7
2	Need more opportunities of religion	36.7
3	Rarely visit the temple	26.7
4	Need of principles in life	26.7
5	Feeling guilty	26.7

This table shows Interested in getting to know God 46.7%, Need more opportunities of religion 36.7%, Rarely visit the temple 26.7%, Need of principles in life 26.7%, Feeling guilty 26.7%.

Table 4.70 Percentage of the most disturbing items among Iraq students in Adapting to academic work problems

No	Items	Iraq Percentage
1	Lack of time for studies	40
2	Lack of interest in books	40
3	Lack of exercise while in high school	36.7
4	Afraid of failing	36.7
5	Lack of systematic programs	33.3

This table shows Lack of time for studies 40%, Lack of interest in books 40%, Lack of exercise while in high school 36.7%, Afraid of failing 36.7%, Lack of systematic programs 33.3%.

Table 4.71 Percentage of the most disturbing items among Iraq students in Future career adapting problems

No	Items	Iraq Percentage
1	Need of planning for the future	66.7
2	Trying to combine marriage and career	56.7
3	Feeling tired due to postponing	50
4	Need of decision about career	50
5	Need of ability to work	50

This table shows need of planning for the future 66.7%, trying to combine marriage and career 56.7%, feeling tired due to postponing 50%, need of decision about career 50%, need of ability to work 50%.

Table 4.72 Percentage of the most disturbing items among Iraqi students in Curriculum and method of teaching problems

No	Items	Iraq Percentage
1	Too many poor lecturers	56.7
2	Lecturers are inefficient in teaching a certain subject	53.3
3	Lecturers are too theoretical	53.3
4	Unable to get required books	50
5	Boring classes	50

This table shows too many poor lecturers 56.7%, lecturers are inefficient in teaching a certain subject 53.3%, lecturers are too theoretical 53.3%, unable to get required books 50%, boring classes 50%.

Table 4.73 Percentage of the most disturbing items among Pakistani students in Health related problems

No	Items	Pakistan Percentage
1	Lack of exercise	50
2	Need medical advise	43.3
3	Digestion problem	40
4	Feeling of fainting	33.3
5	Dental problem	33.3

This table shows lack of exercise 50%, need medical advise 43.3%, digestion problem 40%, feeling of fainting 33.3%, dental problem 33.3%.

Table 4.74 Percentage of the most disturbing items among Pakistani students in Financial, lifestyle and career related problems

No	Items	Pakistan Percentage
1	No stable allowance	90
2	Not sure of future allowance	80
3	Working till late at night	63.3
4	Bored of the same food	63.3
5	Working to support expense	63.3

This table shows no stable allowance 90%, not sure of future allowance 80%, working till late at night 63.3%, bored of the same food 63.3%, working to support expense 63.3%.

Table 4.75 Percentage of the most disturbing items among Pakistani students in Social and recreational problems

No	Items	Pakistan Percentage
1	Willing to improve my thoughts	90
2	Need more opportunity to express myself	83.3
3	Interested in entertaining	76.7
4	Interested in more discussions	73.3
5	Lack of time to enjoy reading	63.3

This table shows willing to improve my thoughts 90%, need more opportunity to express myself 83.3%, interested in entertaining 76.6%, interested in more discussions 73.3%, lack of time to enjoy reading 63.3%.

Table 4.76 Percentage of the most disturbing items among Pakistani students in Psychological social relation problems

No	Items	Pakistan Percentage
1	Lacking behind in most things	86.6
2	Missing someone at home	80
3	Interested in a better personality	70
4	Being afraid and shy	40
5	Stubborn	40

This table shows lacking behind in most things 86.6%, missing someone at home 80%, interested in a better personality 70%, being afraid and shy 40% and stubborn 40%.

Table 4.77 Percentage of the most disturbing items among Pakistani students in Personal relationships and emotional problems

No	Items	Pakistan Percentage
1	Being easily happy	80
2	Thinking seriously about something	73.3
3	Afraid of mistakes	53.3
4	Easily tensed up	50
5	Being worried unnecessarily	46.7

This table shows being easily happy 80%, thinking seriously about something 73.3%, afraid of mistakes 53.3%, easily tensed up 50%, being worried unnecessarily 46.7%.

Table 4.78 Percentage of the most disturbing items among Pakistani students in Marriage and sexual problems

No	Items	Pakistan Percentage
1	Less dates	53.3
2	Could not find a date	53.3
3	Thinking about finding the right person	50
4	No boyfriend/girl friend	46.7
5	Unable to find a suitable place for a date	43.3

This table shows less dates 53.3%, could not find a date 53.3%, thinking about finding the right person 50%, no boyfriend 46.7%, unable to find a suitable place for a date 43.3%.

Table 4.79 Percentage of the most disturbing items among Pakistani students in Family problems

No	Items	Pakistan Percentage
1	Rarely going back home	73.3
2	Parents struggle for me	56.7
3	In need of love and care	53.3
4	Worried about a particular person in the family	50
5	Parents have high expectations	50

This table shows rarely going back home 73.3%, parents struggle for me 56.7%, in need of love and care 53.3%, worried about a particular person in the family 50%, parents have high expectations 50%.

Table 4.80 Percentage of the most disturbing items among Pakistani students in Moral and religious problems

No	Items	Pakistan Percentage
1	Interested in getting to know God	50
2	Need of principles in life	40
3	Remembering the mistakes committed	33.3
4	Rarely visits the temple/church/mosque	30
5	Lose to influence	30

This table shows interested in getting to know God 50%, need of principles in life 40%, remembering the mistakes committed 33.3% rarely visits the temple/church/mosque 30%, lose to influence 30%.

Table 4.81 Percentage of the most disturbing items among Pakistani students in Adapting to academic work problems

No	Items	Pakistan Percentage
1	Easily disturbed while doing a work	43.3
2	Weak in mathematics	43.3
3	Forgotten those learned before	40
4	Having too many out activities	33.3
5	Having problem presenting	33.3

This table shows Easily disturbed while doing a work 43.3%, Weak in mathematics 43.3%, Forgotten those learned before 40%, Having too many out activities 33.3%, Having problem presenting 33.3%.

Table 4.82 Percentage of the most disturbing items among Pakistani students in Future career adapting problems

No	Items	Pakistan Percentage
1	Need of information about career	63.3
2	Choosing a good course for a good career	56.7
3	Need of earlier experience	53.3
4	Need of decision about career	53.3
5	Need of ability to work	53.3

This table shows need of information about career 63.3%, choosing a good course for a good career 56.7%, need of earlier experience 53.3%, need of decision about career 53.3%, need of ability to work 53.3%.

Table 4.83 Percentage of the most disturbing items among Pakistani students in Curriculum and method of teaching problems

No	Items	Pakistan Percentage
1	College is not concerned of students needs	53.3
2	Lack of discussion in class	50
3	Lots of work and assignments	50
4	Too many rules and regulations	50
5	Lecturers are too theoretical	46.7

This table indicates classes are as those in high schools 12.3%, lack of discussion in class 11.6%, too many rules and regulations 11.4%, college is not concerned of students needs 10.4%, lots of work and assignments 9.1%.

4.3 Summary

This chapter represented results of descriptive analysis from the data. As you can see in the table 4.5 which was showed the categories of problems among foreign students the five most highest categories of problems are respectively include: social and recreational problems, financial, life style and career problems, curriculum and method of teaching problems, personal relationships and emotional problems and marriage and sexual problems.

Regarding to the demographical point of view, male students had more problems than females in most of the categories which was discussed in part 4.5 ,most disturbing categories shows by international male students was include (moral and religious problems, health related problems, curriculum and method of teaching problems, marriage and sexual problems and personal relationships and emotional problems). Furthermore regarding to the respondents country of origins, among the selected countries Iranian students have the highest rate of disturbing problems in most of the categories which was discussed in part 4.6, the most highest categories of problems in Iranian students was include (curriculum and method of teaching problems, moral and religious problems, health related problems, marriage and sexual problems and adopting to academic work problems).

CHAPTER 5

DISCUSSION

5.0   Introduction

This chapter is about the discussion, recommendation and limitation of the study regarding the most disturbing category of problems among foreign students in a public University in Malaysia. The discussion is based on research questions.

To identify the most disturbing category of problems faced by foreign students and answer to the research questions the researcher used both quantitative and qualitative method, also Pareto principles used to find the data final results. The questioner consist of two parts, the first part was the demographic information of the respondents, the second part was Shafeq problem checklist (SPCL), since SPCL is consists of eleven categories of problems, Pareto principles was used to identify two most disturbing categories of problems among foreign postgraduate students in the university, the most disturbing category of problems was refer to social and recreational problems and the second main category was related to foreign students financial, life style and career related problems. In on the other hand, the interview was consisting of open-ended questions to explore more details about foreign postgraduate students' problems in each department of the University.

From the total yes given by the respondents to each category of problems the questioner was developed to identify, the most disturbing category of the problems faced by foreign students. The respondents were selected through stratified sampling. There are 354 postgraduate foreign students representative from five countries of origins, which have the highest number of postgraduate students in University. Target respondents of the research were include: 221 respondents from Iran,43 respondents from Indonesia,30 respondents from Nigeria,30 respondents from Iraq and 30 respondents from Pakistan.

5.1 The most disturbing categories of the problems among foreign postgraduate students

Social and recreational problems was the first most disturbing category of problems among foreign students (recreational time is related to the free time to a person, people don't have any necessary work to do in this times and just want to enjoy of their free times, but different people prefer to spend their recreational times by doing different recreational activities and in different ways dependent to their financial and position level (Christopher Pierson, 2001). Social theorists, not only attention to the human needs to studying and working but also they consider the human needs to having leisure times Hunnicutt (1990) believed that leisure as a creative look: He says: "Society must prepare an opportunity for the people to produce creative work and leisure.

On the other hand, according to Plato, human beings always are located in "early stages of Wisdom" (wisdom). They never find truth, Furthermore Hamzeh (2007) done a research and used (MPCL) on (n=16) students regard to the results of the research the first disturbing category of problems among students was recreational problems around 51.5 percent.

Mayes and MCConatha (1982) conduct a research by using MPCL. The results show that the most disturbing problems of the foreign male and female students was in Social and Recreational Activities (SRA). More students in the class of 1986 indicated concerns regarding personal appearance and not having enough time to them. In both classes, men felt awkward making a date more than female, and woman has wanted to improve themselves and travel more than males.

As the results of the research shows the level of recreational problems among foreign students from different country of origins is different, it can be related to the students different cultures and different races prefer to spend their time in different ways (Al Ahmad, 2001).

The second most disturbing category of problems among foreign students was about financial, life style and career related problems. On the other hand providing this needs to the human required spending money and lake of finance or lack of enough financial support for the students can be a challenge to them, because they couldn't provide their basic needs. According to Maslow (1954) if the human needs in the first level doesn't fulfill he couldn't focus to preparing his needs in higher levels such as security, property, health, sexual intimacy, self esteem and confidence.

Worthy et al (2010) report that the most disturbing category of problem among foreign students in Mississippi university (n=450) is their financial behavior, The study shows that the foreign students whose family received public financial helps have higher sensation-seeking score and higher adult status scores have more problematic financial problem in contrast with the students whose family don't receive public assistance.

As the result shows, half of the students have problems about their financial cases, in different aspects and different levels of financial problems among male and female students from different country of origins .According to Worthy et al (2010) financial problem have a direct relative to the age and gender. The older female students have more financial problem.

Sabri et al (2008) conduct a study on foreign students problems (n = 3850) in six public and five private universities. Result shows that the male students have more financial problem than females, most of the respondents had low financial well-being and weakness affect their academic performance.

The research done by Ibrahim et al (2009) on foreign students (n=133) in Kedah campus shows that the degree students have a very poor financial knowledge and they cannot manage their money.

In this study students complain lecturers and supervisor try to financial support for local students but it's clearly appear that the foreign students need more than local students (Nigeria R1). There is no support from the university or supervisors to the students to participate in conferences or publishing a paper (Indonesian R1).

5.2 The most disturbing items in each categories of the problems among foreign postgraduate students

Both qualitative and quantitative results shows that social and recreational problems and financial, lifestyle and career related problems are two most disturbing category of problems faced by foreign students. More than 40 percent of the foreign postgraduate students have problems about their life style, more than 60 percent of them reported that they are bored of the same food.

According to the quantitative findings the most disturbing items in the first disturbing category of problems (social and recreational problems) are as follow: 82.5 percent of foreign students are willing to improve their thoughts, 81.1 percent are interested in vacations, 72 percent need more opportunity to express themselves, 71.5 percent are interested to entertaining and more than 67 percent are interested to improving their thoughts and ethics. They also need more opportunity to express themselves.

The second most disturbing items mentioned by foreign students (financial, lifestyle and career related problems) was as follow: 61.6 percent of the students feel bored of the same food, 58.2 percent express that their working is for their own benefit, 57.9 percent need a part time job, 51.4 percent are not sure of future allowance and 49.4 percent of them are in need of job during holiday.

5.3 The most disturbing items in each categories of the problems among foreign postgraduate students in term of demography

Tendency to have more recreational activity and facilities in university is different in terms of genders. Female students are interested to improve their thoughts and ethnics and also they need more opportunity to express themselves more than males students. More than 80 percent of the males reported that they are interested to vacations but females doesn't show high tendency. On the other hand in contrast to the males more than 60 percent of the females are interested to change their appearance.

About 80 percent of the respondents from different country of origins (Iran, Indonesia, Nigeria, Iraq and Pakistan) are interested to improving their thoughts, but the level of this interest is different in according to their country of origins as follows, Indonesian 93 percent, Pakistanis 90 percent, Iraqi 86.7 percent, Iranians 80.1 percent and Nigerians 66.7 percent (Nigeria R1). This study also showed that more than 60 percent of Iraqis, 80 percent of Indonesians and 60 percent of Iranians are interested to vacations and need more opportunity to express themselves. There is some vocational trips for students in university but this programs are just for local students (Iran R2).

More than 50 percent of the both male and female foreign postgraduate students' need of part time job to support their financial needs and they complained that they are bored of the same food. The males more than 50 percent of the female students express that they need to control of usage money and in contrast with the females. More than 50 percent of the males express that they are in need of job during holidays.The females are more interested to save their money and they

110

are more care about how to spending their money . Males try to spend instead of saving money. They prefer to earn more money and spend it more easily than females (Sabri et al., 2008).

With a short glance to the research results can see that students problems in financial cases also is not completely the same among different country of origins but they also have some similarities in their financial problems, all the foreign students from different country of origins (Iran, Indonesia, Nigeria, Iraq and Pakistan) unanimously are bored of the same food more than 50 percent. Furthermore, more than 50 percent of Indonesian, Iraqis and Nigerian students need part time job and job during holidays.

5.4 Implication

The benefit of this research is the contribution to the body of knowledge, in this research the researcher try to use both qualitative and quantitative method to explore the category of problems. More specific the researcher try to find the most items of each category of problems separated to the gender and country of origins of the students and also the interview was done on ten person one male and on female from each nationality it can be very useful to other researchers who are interested to done multicultural researches on different kind of races and also different genders.

Furthermore through finding the results of this research used Shafeq Problem Check List (SPCL) this inventory is update, modified and its in English version, this specification of this inventory can help the future researchers to doing research with using this inventory on different people from different languages and cultures.

Finally in this research researcher try to introduce Pareto principle and its benefits to summarizing the results thought receiving the more real finding, it will be useful to future researchers who are doing research on the west population and are interested to explore their research finding regarding to more details.

The Shafeq Problem Check List (MPCL) is consist of eleven category and each category is consist of several questions because of this I try to find the most disturbing items in each category to explain. Data collection don during the students' examination time because of this it was difficult to find enough respondents to answering the questions.

5.5 Recommendations

As the societies grow, the new problems arise but if the society want to provide a healthy environment to the residents the principles of the society most try to help the residents to overcome to their problems, the requirement to have a active , healthy society.

Regard to the increase in the number of foreign students in every semester coming to university to continue their study the university faced with numerous problems about the students. University is trying to find the strengths and weakness of the university facilities according to each departments. The university will identify the problem faced by the students and help them to overcome to their problems because the university is going to become a global research university, in order to achieve this the students and university principles and staffs must to do all their effort.

In this research researcher also try to find the most disturbing problems faced by foreign postgraduate students (first most disturbing problem was social and recreational problems and the second most problems was about financial, life style and career related problems).

About the social and recreational problems, most of the students are interested to having time to doing recreational activities besides their studying. For solving this problem university is supposed to improve the suitability of on-campus recreational facilities to the students such as improving the quality of the recreational facilities and recreational equipments. Further more university most try to improve the functionality and adequacy of recreational facilities.

On the other hand, university Unit Sukan department can arrange some scientist and recreational travels for the students in the weekends and holydays and also provide gym rooms near the students hostels that the students could use the facilities during weekends and holydays, because the available gym rooms are close in weekends and holidays.

University can provide recreational workshops and competitions for the students during their holidays such as photography, painting, fishing, bicycle driving, swimming and so on. The university can provide some places to the students, which they could have gathering there and join to each other ,there are such places like this on university campus but there is not enough facility there such as a suitable place to seat, more lights and barbeque to cooking.

Regarding to the students complains about the foods and different tastes of the students from different culture and different country of origins, university can provide special restaurant on-campus that the special foods for each country served on them. To solving the second most disturbing problem faced by foreign students (financial, life style and career related problems) university is supposed to give some loan to students to help them to overcome to their financial problems.

Another suggestion is university can ask the students to participate in some university projects related to the student's course or their research topic and give them salary instead of their cooperation in doing the project. Furthermore, university can ask the top postgraduate students to teach to the degree students or to the students from their same country of origins with their language, according to their teaching ability and their professionalism.

University can provide a situation to the students to investigate their abilities, talents and interests and use of them finding a career. In addition, it can be useful for the students to participate in the workshops related to the career and the ways of saving and managing their money.

5.6 Conclusion

This research was conducted to identify the most disturbing categories of problems among foreign postgraduate students in the university. The research also aimed to examine if there were any differences in term of the respondents gender and country of origins. At the result, the most disturbing category of problems among foreign postgraduate students and also most disturbing items of each category in term of the respondents gender and country of origin was generated.

CHAPTER 6

REFRENCES

Aris Md Safree, Md Yasin and Mariam Adawiah Dzulkifli, *(2009). DIFFERENCES IN PSYCHOLOGICAL PROBLEMS BETWEEN LOW AND HIGH ACHIEVING STUDENTS*, The Journal of Behavioral Science 4(1).

Basiron, B., Muhamad, A. Mustari M.I. (2007), *Kepentingan Dasar Pengasingan Mengikut Gender Bagi Mengatasi Masalah Sosial di kalangan Mahasiswa, Simposium* Pengajaran Pembelajaran UTM.

Burkes, C.M. (1995). the *adjustment problems of African – American undergraduate students studying at west Virginia university* (Morgantown). Dissertation abstracts international, 56 (11)

Chong Abdullah, M. (2009). Adjusment among First Year Students in a Malaysian University. *European Journal of Social Sciences, 8.*

Day, R.C., Hajj, F.M. (1986). *Supporting International Student Adjustment experience of the Americana University of Beirut.* Journal of College Student Personnel.

Dahlia I., Rabitah H. and Zuraidah , (2009), Mohamed Isa3, A Study on *Financial Literacy of Malaysian Degree Students, Cross-cultural Communication 5(4).*

Fadi Maher, Saleh Al-Khasawneh (2010), *WRITING FOR ACADEMIC PURPOSES: PROBLEMS FACED BY ARAB POSTGRADUATE STUDENTS OF THE COLLEGE OF BUSINESS, UUM* , ESP World (28), Volume 9(2).

Fromm, E. (1990). *The Sane Socity.* Holt Paperbacks.

Ghanem, Mohammad bagi, (2008). *How the students spend their Recreational time* in Islamic University of Iran shiraz.

Ginsberg, H.R. (1980). *reported problems of rural students at the university of pensilvania as a function of gender and class.* Dissertation Abstracts international, 41 (10)

Hatman, B.J. (1968*). A survey of college students problems identified by the Mooney problem checklist.psychological reports* (22), 715-716

Hamzeh, H.B. (2007). *Hubungan Kategori Masalah Dengan Demografi pelajar-pelajar tingkatan empat di sekolah menengah Zon pasir Gudang berasakan Money problem checklist.* Master thesis. UTM, Skudai

Kenny, (1986). the *extent and function of parental attachment among first-year college students.* Jurnal of youth and adolescence, 16(1)

Kenny, (*1986). Acculturation level, perceived English fluency, perceived social support level, and depression among Taiwanese international students,* College Student Journal ,Magazine/Journal Subject.

Koplik, E,K, and devito, A.J (1986). *problems of freshmen: comparison of classes of 1976 and 1986.*jurnal of college student personnel (27), 124-131

Krejcie, R.V. and Morgan, D.W. (1970). *Determining sample size research,educational and psychological measurement.* (30), 607-610.

Lipovetsky, S. (2009). Pareto 80/20 law: derivation via random partitioning. *International Journal of Mathematical Education in Science and Technology, 40*(2), 271 – 277.

Lee, (1997). *NEW DIRECTIONS FOR TEACHING AND LEARNING,* no. 70, Summer 1997. Jossey-Bass Publishers

Lee, Kuang – wu , (2000) . *A comparative analysis of foreign students needs in Taiwan.*

Mayes, A.N. and McConatha, J.(1982). *surveying students services.* Journal of college students personel (23), 473-476

Maslow, A. (1968). *Toward a Psychology of Being* (2end ed.). New York: Van Nostrand Reinhold.

Maureen E Kenny, (1986) *the extent and function of personal attachment among first-year collage students,* journal of youth and adolescents , 16(1)

Poorshaghaghi 1992, *Counseling, Mental Health Services.* Speaks: Farsi. Education: George Washington University,

Peng,T.W. (2006). *Hubungan Kategori masalah dengan demografi di antara pelajar tahun satu di fakulti pengurusan dan pembangunan sumber manusia. Master thesis.* University Teknologi Malaysia,skudai, johor

Rojek, Chris and Susan M. (2006) *The History of Western Leisure"* in A Handbook of Leisure Studies, edited by Show, Palgrave, Macmillan.

Rosenthal, D., Russell, J., Thomson, G. (2008). *The health and wellbeing of international students at an Australian university.* Higher Education, 55(1): 51-67

Rotter, J. (1954). *Social learning and clinical psychology.* New York: Prentice-Hall.

Russell, J., Thomson, G., & Rosenthal, D. (2008). *International student use of university health and counselling services.* Higher Education, 56(1), 59-75.

Sabri, Macdonald, Masud, Paim, Tahira k., Othman, (2008). *Financial Behavior and Problems among College Students in Malaysia: Research and Education Implication* . Consumer Interests Annual. 54.

Sawir, Marginson, Deumert, Nyland, Ramia (2007) *Loneliness and International Students: An Australian Study.* Journal of Studies in International Education, DOI: 10.1177/1028315307299699 .

Shafeq, S. M. (2008). *Shafeq Problem Check List (SPCL)*

Sheahila, S. (2008).*Hubungan kategori masalah dengan demografi pelajar-pelajar tingkatan empat di sekolah menengah daerah kota tingi berasakan (money problem checklist),* master thesis, UTM,skudai

Sherry, M., Thomas, P., Chui, W. (2010*). International students: a vulnerable student population.* Higher Education, 60(1): 33-46

Sing, C. M., M. Fadzil Che Din dan Laily Mastura Harun (2004). *Level of Phsychological stress Among College student in Malaysia.* Kertas Kerja Seminar Kaunseling: UUM.

Su, A.B. (2004). *satu tinjauam mengenai kategori masalah yang dihadapi oleh pelajar kemasukan terus di kolej 13*, UTM. Master thesis, skudai

Terri and Fisher, (1986). *family communication and sexual behavior and attitudes of collage students*, journal of youth and adolescents , 16(5) .

Tinto, Vincent (1987). *Leaving College: Rethinking the Causes and Cures of Student Attrition. Chicago*: The University of Chicago Press.

UTM. (2011). About UTM. Retrieved 10 February 2011, from http://www.utm.my/aboututm/about-utm.html

Worthy, S., Jonkman, J., Blinn-Pike, L. (2010). *Sensation-Seeking, Risk-Taking, and Problematic Financial Behaviors of College Students.* Journal of Family and Economic Issues, 31(2): 161-170

CHAPTER 7

APPENDIX: QUESTIONNAIRE

RESEARCH ON PROBLEMS FACED BY FOREIGN
STUDENTS IN A PUBLIC UNIVERSITY IN MALAYSIA

Dear students,

The objective of this questionnaire is to identify problems faced by foreign students who are currently studying at a public University in Malaysia.

Please answer Part A and B of this questionnaire. Part A is regarding the demography and Part B is regarding the problems by categories.

Your cooperation in participating in the survey will assist university to provide better   supports and services to you.

Thank you

Atefeh Kamankesh

Part A: Demography

Please tick (√) with appropriate answer.

Gender   Female (   )   Male (   )

1) Age   (   ) Years old

2) Nationality (Country of origin) _____

3) Marital status   Single (   )   Married (   )

4) Semester of being studying at UTM

   Semester 1 (   )   Semester 2 (   )

   Semester 3 (   )   Semester 4 (   )

Part B: Problems by Categories

Please tick (√) the appropriate box either Yes or No.

1) Health Related Problems

No	Items	Yes	No
1	Easily tired out		
2	Lack of exercise		
3	Lack of sleep		
4	Allergy (fever, asthma rashes and others)		
5	Easily stressed out and headache		
6	Not alluring physical appearance		
7	Often having sore throat		
8	Often having flu		
9	Sinus problem		
10	Bad vision		
11	Frequent headache		
12	Menstruation problem		
13	Feeling of fainting		
14	Digestion problem		
15	Dental problem		
16	Need medical advise		

2) Financial, Lifestyle and Career Related Problems

No	Items	Yes	No
17	Lack of finance for clothing		
18	Less financial support from family		
19	Lack of finance compared to friends		
20	Poor of finance management		
21	Need of part-time job		
22	Too many financial problems		
23	In need of money for better health		
24	Need to control usage of money		
25	Family worried about finance		
26	Dislike financial support from others		
27	Working till late at night		
28	Transportation problem		
29	Lack of privacy in residing area		
30	No entertainment with friends		
31	No satisfaction and diet		
32	Bored of the same food		
33	Lack of finance		
34	No stable allowance		
35	Not sure of future allowance		
36	In need of job during holiday		
37	Working to support expense		
38	Working is for my own benefit		

3) Social and Recreational Problems

No	Items	Yes	No
39	Lack of recreations		
40	Lack of exercising opportunities		
41	Lack of time for art and music		
42	Lack of opportunities for entertainment		
43	Lack of time for myself		
44	Inefficient use of free time		
45	Willing to improve my thoughts		
46	Need more opportunity to express myself		
47	Uncomfortable in meeting people		
48	Uncomfortable during dates		
49	Late in communicating with others		
50	Lack of involvement in student activities		
51	Boring weekends		
52	Interested in dancing		
53	Interested in entertaining		
54	Interested in changing appearance		
55	Interested in improving ethics		
56	Facing difficulties in continuing a conversation		
57	Lack of sports skills		
58	Lack of opportunities in enjoying the environment		
59	Lack of opportunity to continue a hobby		
60	Lack of time to enjoy reading		
61	Interested in more discussions		
62	Lack of opportunities to enjoy own interests		
63	Lack of social life		
64	No enjoyment during holidays		
65	Interested in vacations		

4) Psychological Social Relation Problems

No	Items	Yes	No
66	Being afraid and shy		
67	Easily embarrassed		
68	Feeling uncomfortable with others		
69	Missing someone at home		
70	Interested in a better personality		
71	Lacking behind in most things		
72	Easily hurt		
73	Ill-talked		
74	Worried about being nice to others		
75	Worried how I captivate other people		
76	Feeling lost		
77	Jealous		
78	Stubborn		
79	Acting without thinking		
80	Being childish		
81	Hating someone		
82	Being hated by someone		
83	No one understand me		
84	Difficulty in expressing oneself		
85	Easily hurt others feelings		
86	Avoid oneself from those that you hate		
87	Easily influenced by others		
88	In need of money for better health		
89	Lack of leadership skills		

5) Personal Relationships and Emotional Problems

No	Items	Yes	No
90	Thinking seriously about something		
91	Being worried unnecessarily		
92	Being uncomfortable		
93	Being easily happy		
94	Bad mood		
95	Failure in everything that you wish to do		
96	Easily give up		
97	Usually unhappy		
98	Daydreaming		
99	Forgetful		
100	Easily tensed up		
101	Easily angered		
102	Careless		
103	Lazy		
104	Likes to create stories		
105	Not being serious		
106	Afraid of mistakes		
107	Unable to make decisions		
108	Lack of confidence		
109	Unable to forget bad experiences		
110	Feels that life is not perfect		
111	Too many personal problems		
112	Easily broken down		

6) Marriage and Sexual Problems

No	Items	Yes	No
113	Less dates		
114	Could not find a date		
115	Unable to find a suitable place for a date		
116	Taking decision to maintain a relationship		
117	Afraid of losing the one you love		
118	Loving someone who does not love you		
119	Too strict in sex related issues		
120	Thinking about finding the right person		
121	Being in love		
122	Figuring out if I am in love		
123	Thinking of the future prospect person		
124	Shy to talk about sex		
125	Disturbance about ideas of sex		
126	Need of information about sex		
127	Thinking about getting information with another sex		
128	Love failure		
129	No boyfriend, girlfriend		
130	Thinking if I will ever get married		
131	Thinking too much about sex		
132	Easily agitated		
133	Taking a long time to get married		
134	Need of advice about marriage		
135	Thinking if the marriage will succeed		

7) Family Problems

No	Items	Yes	No
136	Parents struggle for me		
137	Worried about a particular person in the family		
138	Frequent quarrels in family		
139	Unhappy of a particular behavior		
140	Cannot discuss about a problem at home		
141	Clash of opinions at home		
142	Going opposite parents wishes		
143	Parents have high expectations		
144	Having a huge responsibility		
145	Do not share everything with parents		
146	Parents do most of the decision		
147	Need of more freedom		
148	In need of love and care		
149	Rarely going back home		

8) Moral and Religious Problems

No	Items	Yes	No
150	Rarely visit the mosque, temple or church		
151	Need of principles in life		
152	Need more opportunities of religion		
153	Interested in understanding the Quran, Bible		
154	Interested in getting to know God		
155	Confused about moral values		
156	Lying without intention		
157	Pretending		
158	Having bad habits		
159	Unable to leave bad habits		
160	Not honest		
161	Feeling guilty		
162	Remembering the mistakes committed		
163	Lose to influence		
164	Lack of self-defense		

11) Curriculum and Method of Teaching Problems

No	Items	Yes	No
209	Unable to get required books		
210	College is not concerned of students needs		
211	Boring classes		
212	Too many poor lecturers		
213	Lecturers are inefficient in teaching a certain subject		
214	Lecturer has a bad personality		
215	Lack of a good college advisor		
216	Lack of one to one help from lecturers		
217	Lack of opportunity to speak to lecturers		
218	Lecturers are not interested in students		
219	Lecturers are not concerned about student's feelings		
220	Lack of discussion in class		
221	Classes are as those in high schools		
222	Lots of work and assignments		
223	Lecturers are too theoretical		
224	Teaching is inefficient		
225	Subjects are not related to course		
226	Too many rules and regulations		
227	Unable to get the wanted course		
228	Unfair grades		
229	Unfair tests		
230	Poor arrangement of campus activities		
231	Less lively campus		
232	Campus is lack of recreational facilities		

www.ingramcontent.com/pod-product-compliance
Lightning Source LLC
Chambersburg PA
CBHW070146290526
45789CB00002B/645